How to Open & Operate a Financially Successful

Floral and Florist

Business Both Online and Off

By Stephanie Beener

How to Open & Operate a Financially Successful Floral and Florist Business Both Online and Off — With Companion CD-ROM

ISBN-13: 978-1-60138-140-8   ISBN-10: 1-60138-140-9

Library of Congress Cataloging-in-Publication Data

Beener, Stephanie N., 1983-
  How to open & operate a financially successful florist and floral
business both online and off : with companion cd-rom / by Stephanie N.
Beener.
    p. cm.
  Includes bibliographical references and index.
  ISBN-13: 978-1-60138-140-8 (alk. paper)
  ISBN-10: 1-60138-140-9 (alk. paper)
  1. Florists. 2. Flowers--Marketing. I. Title. II. Title: How to open
and operate a financially successful florist and floral business both
online and off.

  SB443.B44 2008
  745.92068--dc22
                    2008028130

INTERIOR LAYOUT DESIGN: Vickie Taylor • vtaylor@atlantic-pub.com

Printed on Recycled Paper

Printed in the United States

We recently lost our beloved pet "Bear," who was not only our best and dearest friend but also the "Vice President of Sunshine" here at Atlantic Publishing. He did not receive a salary but worked tirelessly 24 hours a day to please his parents. Bear was a rescue dog that turned around and showered myself, my wife Sherri, his grandparents Jean, Bob and Nancy and every person and animal he met (maybe not rabbits) with friendship and love. He made a lot of people smile every day.

We wanted you to know that a portion of the profits of this book will be donated to The Humane Society of the United States.

–Douglas & Sherri Brown

THE HUMANE SOCIETY
OF THE UNITED STATES©

The human-animal bond is as old as human history. We cherish our animal companions for their unconditional affection and acceptance. We feel a thrill when we glimpse wild creatures in their natural habitat or in our own backyard.

Unfortunately, the human-animal bond has at times been weakened. Humans have exploited some animal species to the point of extinction.

The Humane Society of the United States makes a difference in the lives of animals here at home and worldwide. The HSUS is dedicated to creating a world where our relationship with animals is guided by compassion. We seek a truly humane society in which animals are respected for their intrinsic value, and where the human-animal bond is strong.

Want to help animals? We have plenty of suggestions. Adopt a pet from a local shelter, join The Humane Society and be a part of our work to help companion animals and wildlife. You will be funding our educational, legislative, investigative and outreach projects in the U.S. and across the globe.

Or perhaps you'd like to make a memorial donation in honor of a pet, friend or relative? You can through our Kindred Spirits program. And if you'd like to contribute in a more structured way, our Planned Giving Office has suggestions about estate planning, annuities, and even gifts of stock that avoid capital gains taxes.

Maybe you have land that you would like to preserve as a lasting habitat for wildlife. Our Wildlife Land Trust can help you. Perhaps the land you want to share is a backyard—that's enough. Our Urban Wildlife Sanctuary Program will show you how to create a habitat for your wild neighbors.

So you see, it's easy to help animals. And The HSUS is here to help.

The Humane Society of the United States
2100 L Street NW
Washington, DC 20037
202-452-1100
www.hsus.org

Table of Contents

Preface

Although it seems to be all smiles and buckets of flowers, the floral industry has some fierce competition. Many businesses go under because owners were not prepared for what the industry threw at them after they opened. This book will help you learn the many aspects of the trade to prevent the same from happening to you. It is wise to learn as much as you can about every aspect of floral commerce before opening your doors. For starters, you must make sure this industry is for you. A common misconception is that working with flowers is a breeze. Although it is fun, it is also extremely hard work and shop owners must be determined and willing to sacrifice many hours when they first open. There are also many other sides to the business that might have little to do with working with flowers. You also must determine whether there is a market and whether you can specialize with a specific niche to make your company more lucrative. Before opening, it is always wise to be educated so you will understand the different aspects of business, finance, accounting, legal matters, employees, customer service, suppliers, your shop, and product care. This book will introduce you to all the basic ideas and concepts you will need to start your own business. Keep reading to learn more about the floral industry.

Is This for You?

Getting Started

There are many things florists do on a daily basis, and many they do on a periodic one. Before you decide whether this business is for you, you need to get to know the basic ins and outs of how it is run. It is certainly not all just flowers and arranging. A large portion of getting into the floral business is having savvy business knowledge. You will need to develop business and marketing plans. You will also need to have a firm grasp on financing and accounting. Management skills are a necessity, especially if you plan on having employees. You must also have strong customer service skills. A basic knowledge of the legalities that can occur when dealing with people and business is essential. Having an eye on the future and knowing where you would like to head is also ideal. As you can see, there is much to do and learn before beginning a career in the floral industry. We will touch on all these issues and more throughout this book.

Types of Floral Businesses

Retail

Retail is the most common, and probably the most sought after, career in the floral industry. When opening a retail shop, there are a few factors to consider before making your final decisions.

You will want to begin by scoping out a perfect location to open. In every small town, there is a flower shop located on the main street that has been around forever. Locals know it by heart, and this is the competition. Proximity to competition should factor into your chosen site. You do not want to be so close that you go under because loyal locals always choose this landmark over your new store, but you do not want to be so far out of town that you cannot get any business. You might also want to ask yourself if there is enough business for both of you. Finding your own spot, where you will be the sole shop and there is enough market to truly make your business take off, is ideal.

Although most flower shops are on a main street in town, you should consider all the options. Take a look at properties on the main street versus properties a few blocks off. Choose one that suits your budget in the most appropriate manner. When looking at properties, whether renting or buying, you must also keep in mind all the equipment that must fit into it. Figuring in the display space, refrigerated sections, work space, and storage should all play a part in choosing the site. If you simply cannot afford a large space, consider renting a storage unit a few minutes from your store, which will enable easy and quick access. Prices on storage units range from a few dollars a month to big dollar spots; try to find one in your price range. Keep a record of everything that is placed into storage so that you only have to make one or two stops a day to pick up supplies.

Besides the location and equipment, you will also want to think about the atmosphere you would like to provide. When a customer walks through the door of your store, you want the ambience of the atmosphere you have created to envelop them. When creating the environment inside your shop, think about the location. If you are located in the countryside, a country theme would be ideal. If you are on a mainline in the city, a more high-end, upscale feeling will work best. Whatever you choose, make sure it plays into the image you want people to remember when they leave your store. Create a "look" and include it on every marketing aspect of your business, such as signage and business cards. This will ensure that the impression your customers get when they walked into your store will be with them whenever they look at your business card or see marketing for your store.

In Short: Although you may know that you want to work in the industry, be aware of exactly what you are getting yourself into. You might think you want to cut fresh flowers each day in a retail shop, but after opening up, you might find yourself wishing you would have followed your gut and gone into supplies instead. Do what will work best for you by taking your own personality and well-being into consideration.

Wholesale Florist

Wholesale is a business of perishables. If you plan on opening a wholesale operation, you must be prepared to work around the flowers' schedules. Wholesalers must get up very early to get the best picks at the flower markets. You will also need to be organized and efficient to pick the right quantities for your retailers. Since you will most likely be dropping off the fresh flowers directly at your buyers' doors, you will be unloading a majority of your picks before they ever reach your warehouse.

Your warehouse space does not need to be huge. It should, though, be large enough to provide plenty of storage for some excess inventory. You should always have extra flowers available for retail customers that have last-minute orders and walk-ins, as they can only store so much. If they know you always have backup, your relationship will become more fruitful.

Your shop should also have office space, because it is a good place to store business and inventory records. It is also a nice, quiet spot where you can come up with marketing ideas and stock marketing materials. Keeping a computer on-hand is an advantage. This will allow access to research on other competitors, retailers, or flowers you would like to purchase. In today's world, having a Web site is almost a necessity, and a personal computer will allow you the freedom to create your own. Computers are also handy for storing records so that physical files do not take up needed space. They can also take orders, although you will also still want to take orders by hand.

Another big component to wholesaling is refrigeration. Your customers depend on the flowers to be kept fresh for their customers. If your refrigeration is not 100 percent reliable, your customers will lose their customers. You will also begin to feel the loss on your end. To prevent that from happening, make sure you have a refrigerator truck to carry materials; it is the only way to keep flowers fresh on the journey. Get the truck tuned up regularly so that it is always in good working condition.

You also need refrigerated storage in your store for the previously mentioned excess flower stock you will need to keep. You will not need much — just enough to get by for those last minute calls. Over time, you will see trends in which kinds of flowers you will need to store in your warehouse, such as roses, which retailers often sell out of on a daily basis.

If you are going into wholesale, you must be able to stand behind your product. You can do so by:

- Ensuring deliveries are on time every time

- Being flexible with your customers

- Providing discounts for large or bulk orders

- Constantly seeking and introducing new products to keep customers interested

- Continually researching so you can educate customers on new flowers and plants

- ❀ Making yourself available to customers

- ❀ Holding a meeting with new customers so they can inspect your product themselves and ask questions

- ❀ Keeping retailers interested by hosting events so they can see your product firsthand, which allows for curious potential customers to meet you and see what you are all about

- ❀ Trying to market yourself jointly with retailers, so you can split the bill, ads become cheaper, and your name gets out there

- ❀ Keeping everything fresh in your business (take note that your customers are also running a business; no retailer wants a stagnant relationship, and neither do you

Statistic %   According to the Society of American Florists, nearly 70 percent of U.S. grown flowers sold in floral shops come from California.

Greenhouse

Greenhouse owners find many advantages and disadvantages in this line of the floral business. If you live in a warmer climate, your stock can work year-round and you can often grow and sell nearly any type of flower. Conversely, if you live in a climate where the winters are harsh, you might have to close up shop for a few months until it warms up again. There are always ways to make a greenhouse business work for you. Keep busy and non-busy times in mind. During busy times, such as spring when landscapers and homeowners alike will be busting down your door, you will want to make sure you have plenty of stock for anyone who comes around. During slower times, you can switch inventory over to suit the holidays. Have pumpkins and hay bales for Halloween and Thanksgiving, and Christmas flowers available for the winter holidays. If your shop often gets so slow that you need to close down in the winter, you can rethink your strategy and add supply stock, such as pots, seeds, soil, tools, and garden furniture. In the greenhouse business, where there is a will, there is often a way.

In Short: According the U.S. Department of Labor, in 2006, total sales of greenhouse and nursery crops in the United States totaled nearly $52 million, yet the number of producers dropped to 6,546 in 2006 from 7,178 in 2005. Fewer growers are making bigger bucks.

Wholesale Floral Supplies

If you love flowers but do not have a green thumb, you can always get into the wholesale floral supplies side of the market. The supplies side is often a win-win situation for owners. You do not have to deal with daily store life, such as customer walk-ins, like a retailer does. You also do not have to worry about perishable product constantly. You can use your creative juices when choosing stock. You can open up a store to sell supplies to the public or you can maintain a warehouse. Choices are limitless.

Practical Pointer

If you are still in school or do not plan on opening your business for quite some time, it never hurts to get some hands-on experience in an established shop. You can still keep your day job, but spend an evening or two a week soaking up practical knowledge that will be useful in your future.

For wholesale suppliers, the location of the store is not as important as in a retail shop. You want to be close enough that getting last-minute items to a customer is not a burden, but you can save some money by having a warehouse off the main street. Make sure the warehouse is not dingy but is bright and cheery. You and your employees, if you choose to have one or two, will be there stocking, shipping, taking inventory, and answering customer phone calls nearly every day. Make sure the warehouse is dressed accordingly. Your customers will not want dirty supplies, so make sure you take the time to clean up weekly. You might also consider having an annual clearance sale at the same time each year that all of your customers know about. This way, you can get rid of supplies that have not been moved out of the warehouse to make room for new items.

You will need to maintain outstanding relationships with retail store owners. Making sure you always have basic florist needs — such as wire, foam, glue, boxes, and paper — is imperative. You will need to stock classic and timeless items, but you can also use your creativity to seek out fun, unique vases and other decorative pieces. Have a wide variety for your customers and be flexible. If you pay attention to what your customers want and always have plenty of it for them, wholesale floral supplies can be lucrative in the floral business.

Is There a Market or Niche For You?

Any business minded person knows that to open up your own company, you have to have a market, and having a niche within that market is even better.

Statistic According to the Society of American Florists, at the turn of the century nearly 26,200 floral businesses made an annual average of $250,000 each.

You must determine whether there is a feasible customer base within your targeted market and location. Much of how you go about figuring out where you stand has to do with what type of retail business you are looking to get into. If you are trying to break into the retail business, you will have to consider other floral shops around you and whether it is worth it to try to move into their more established market. If you are planning on opening a wholesale business for flowers or supplies, you will have to seek out retail florists and ensure there is enough business. You will also have to see if there is any interest by any of the retailers, since they might already have a relationship with another wholesale company. If you want to operate a greenhouse, you will have to take the weather into consideration. You might also want to think about how many other greenhouses are around and whether it seems that your target location could use your services. For example, are there mainly condos around who, under association contract, cannot maintain their own yards, or are there many large communities filled with owners who do their own gardening?

While you are figuring this out, do not be afraid to ask

questions. Go to local businesses, such as funeral homes or wedding sites, and ask whom they use and whom the majority of their customers use. Tell them you want to open a floral business and evaluate whether they seem interested or not. It is not a bad idea to gather a list of customers, if you can, and call around to see whether they would be interested in meeting with you to discuss buying their supplies or flowers from you. This is an especially good idea for wholesalers.

Once you have formed an idea of what the market is in your chosen location, you should be able to see whether your business will be a success. If you choose to stay within this market, you might also want to research a niche. A niche is a specialized part of the retail industry, such as funeral arrangements or wedding flowers. While you gather information on your location, check into this as well. If you can figure out what type of niche your location is missing, you can make your business more lucrative by adding this missing link for your customers. You must make sure before opening whether your business idea or specific niche will be worth your time.

Education and Experience

In the Business

There is no better way to gain knowledge in the floral industry than with hands-on experience. If you know you want this to be your career path, working in the business as early as possible is the best way to go. Interview with different companies, as you do not have to work for someone who has a shop identical to the one you want to open.

Working for a store that has a different atmosphere than what you plan on creating might work to your advantage. You already have a thought of whom you want your ideal customer to be, but it never hurts to learn about other customers within the industry and what they want out of their local retailer. Make sure you are honest with your new employer. Let him or her know you plan on opening up a floral business in the future. More often than not, a new employer will welcome the idea. They know that you will be dedicated, hard working, and willing to learn since you are not just there for a paycheck, but for the experience of it all. Try to get a job that is out of the region where you would like your store location to be. This way, you will not have to compete against your employer in the future. They will see you are going out of your way as a courtesy, and should be more than willing to help you soak up as much knowledge as you can before you go on your way.

Be sure to try everything — vendor relations, customer service, arranging, ordering, and anything else that might be thrown your way. Go above and beyond. Clean, organize, care for flowers, offer to do deliveries, or design a window display. When you open your own business, you will be happy you have the experience under your belt.

College

Although it is not necessary, having a degree in the floral business can be helpful. It may get you a position over someone else who does not have one, but that is not why it is important. You might want to get a degree so you can learn about the business, financial, and marketing sides of the industry — things you may not be able to get into by simply working in the industry. Having this education will help you setup your own business plan and better organize your financial situation.

In Short: Classes are often available at local colleges. Soak up as much business and marketing information as you can before opening your own business.

There are hundreds of floral schools, not only in the United States, but around the world. If you can afford it and you have the time, going to a school outside of the United States will expand your horizons and allow you to see a market you might not have been able to otherwise. Just be sure that this school offers business savvy ideas you will be able to use when you return to home base.

There are plenty of schools within the United States that will supply you with all the information you will need. Here are some wonderful examples:

Floral Design Institute

> The ActivSpace Building
> 1500 NW 18th Avenue, Suite 109
> Portland, OR 97209

or

> The Maritime Building
> 911 Western Avenue, Suite 575
> Seattle, WA 98104

This school offers two locations in the northwestern United States. With over 1,000 students each year, the

Floral Design Institute offers students hands-on learning experiences with many types of flowers and foliage. They also offer distance learning and special training programs.

Trim International Floral School

4800 Dahlia Street
Denver, CO 80216
Ph: 800-858-9854

or

4725 Lumber Avenue N.E.
Suite 4
Albuquerque, NM 87019
Ph: 800-786-2640

This school focuses on the "building blocks learning manner." It is the most simplified way to learn about flowers and foliage since one lesson builds upon the previous one until schooling is complete. Trim is also recognized by the American Institute of Floral Designers (AIFD).

South Florida Center for Floral Studies

360 South Congress Avenue
West Palm Beach, FL 33406
Ph: 800-765-8523

This school, located in sunny Florida, boasts a curriculum that rounds out many aspects of the business including arranging, marketing, business, and advanced knowledge classes for seasoned florists.

Connecticut Florists Association (CFA)

Conngreen@aol.com

CFA offers two different educational courses. They have the CFA Floral Design School, which is open to anybody who wants to join. They also feature the CFA School, which is a series of continuing education programs for people in the industry only. The school is also licensed by the Connecticut Department of Higher Education.

There are also many community colleges that offer courses in marketing, business, and finances that will help you round out your business sense.

Online

If you do not have the time or means to attend regular classes, you can also achieve certification status through online programs. Here are a few examples of online schools you can attend for your floral certification.

Ashworth University: This program has a well-rounded curriculum which includes courses on how to develop your creativity and render your own unique sense of style; basics like harmony, color, shapes and rhythm; foliage and flowers for specific occasions; caring for plants; and how to express certain emotions through your creations. You do not need to have any prior experience or prerequisites.

Penn Foster Career School: This school includes everything you need to know, whether you want to simply work at a floral shop or own one.

Stratford Career Diploma: Stratford offers distance education programs that show you everything from arranging, to financials, to marketing in order to ensure your entry into the floral industry will be a success.

It seems as though there are just as many online schools as there are brick ones, so make sure you do your research and select the one that is best for you.

Continuing Education

There are many local vendors and events in major cities that will help you with your continuing education. Whether you attend flower shows, seminars, or events thrown by other florists, you will continue to learn and expand your horizons within your business. Try to attend at least one national floral convention annually in a major city to make sure you are seeing the best of the best and keeping up with trends.

After establishing what part of the flower and foliage market you would like to get into, doing research, figuring out whether there is a market and a niche for you, and becoming educated and confident in your business sense, you are well on your way to a career in one of the most booming industries in the nation.

"When words escape, flowers speak."

Bruce W. Currie

Marketing Research

Room for Your Business?

With marketing, the first research you want to do is to find out where your customers are going to come from and what other businesses like yours are in the area.

The first thing you need to do is vie for the perfect location. As you have probably seen, most floral shops are located on the main street of the town they are in. This is no accident. Just the visual appeal of a busy street alone helps attract customers. When considering locations, make sure it is in a visible spot along a highly traveled road. A town where there is no other flower shop is your best bet for gaining the most revenue.

After you have settled on a general location, you will have to consider the building that you want to be in. Most buildings in the center of a town or city have apartments above them. If this makes you uneasy, try looking toward the outskirts of town for a single building. If you want to be right in the mix, look for a building that has the general amenities you need — a front room (for customers), a back room (for preparation), a storage area, and a bathroom. An ideal store would also include a store front so you can display your arrangements for passersby to see.

When on the hunt for your store location, try looking at places that require minimal work to save money. A real score would be acquiring an old flower shop that includes everything you need. An empty shell is ideal since you can add on as necessary. If all you can find is an old restaurant or something similar, that will also work. You will just have to keep in mind that now you will not only encounter the normal flower shop fees like coolers, you will quite possibly have to overhaul the entire location.

The location you want to open your business in must have enough customers to support your revenue and other floral businesses in the same vicinity. If there is not enough business, rather than trying to compete with an established store, you might want to think about a new site. If you are the only floral shop in town, or one of a few, it is always smart to keep an eye out for new competition. Join your local chamber of commerce so you can find out what you need to know about newcomers. This is also a great way to meet other local business owners and create a rapport with potential customers.

In Short: Although the first few months, or even years, may seem like a whirlwind, make sure you attend all meetings for any associations, business groups, or chambers of commerce you have joined. These meetings can often provide you with essential business information, a source of networking, a way to gain a sense of community, and a link to potential customers. These are meetings you cannot afford to pass up due to a busy schedule.

When you are figuring out whether there is enough revenue for your store, and possibly for surrounding competitors, you might want to take the price range you are willing to offer and compare it with your target customers income averages. You want to make sure these match. You do not want to offer flowers that are too high for your target market's budget, but you also do not want to offer flowers that are priced too low in a high-class neighborhood. Flowers or supplies priced too low may lead upper class clients to believe that quality is lacking.

There are normally three kinds of customers — walk-in, call-in, and special markets. You will want to make sure your location adheres to all three. You want to be in a spot with foot traffic so that passersby might be tempted to stop in. You will also want to make your phone number visible on signage and on any other marketing tools you are using so that call-ins do not have to dig for your number. Making sure there are plenty of other businesses, such as funeral homes and churches that use floral services often, is ideal. If your location is filled with different types of businesses, be sure you wiggle into a chosen niche or two. If you see that there are many wedding and special event sites around, use it to your advantage and learn all you can about these particular niches. Attend some of these events and talk with people to learn what they want and to spread word of your endeavors.

Competition

There are plenty of reasons that customers become loyal to one florist over another. One of the main reasons is the owners and employees. Make sure that each customer's experience is a good one. If for some reason a customer is not pleased, figure out how you could have made it better to avoid the same mistake in the future. You can also do the same type of research with similar businesses in your area. Examine them. Go into the shop. Order their flowers each way you can — walk-in, call-in, and special order — and see what makes them tick from a customer's point of view. Use your good and bad experiences to your advantage to avoid making the same blunders with your own customers. You will also want to try to distinguish yourself from the rest of the pack. Once you have seen the inside of your competitors' stores, tweak your own so its uniqueness stands out in the crowd.

Practical Pointer

Always be aware of what is going on in the community where your shop is located. Knowing about a new competitor, a new law for retail store owners, or even a new neighborhood going up around your store as soon as possible will be to your advantage. Join your local chamber of commerce and befriend other retail store owners, no matter what industry they are in. Gossip aside, you will learn interesting information that you might not have been in tune to otherwise.

Customer Base

Practice good judgment when you are trying to pull in clients. Do not "steal" customers from your competitors. You can make enticing offers to locals through advertisements and marketing schemes, but it is not wise to stand in front of another floral shop handing out coupons or fliers for your own store.

Use family, friends, and other acquaintances as automatic customers. You can use their web of family and friends to further expand your customer base. Try to use any opportunity as a business one. If you do decide to join a class at your local college, ask classmates to use your shop. If you join your local chamber of commerce or Small Business Administration (SBA), attend meetings in your genre and others. Hand out business cards every time you go. Any chance meeting can be used to your advantage when you are trying to create a loyal customer base.

You can also pull in customers with marketing tactics such as an advertisement in the Sunday paper. You can do mailings to local office buildings, businesses, and residences that may find your niche practical and useful. Ask current customers where they often go when they are out and about so you can be sure to post ads or signage to catch a potential client's eye. The only limitation is your own creativity.

After you have done research on the competition and customer base, use logic to determine whether this is the market for you. If not, move on to the next town and try again. If so, you can start to develop your marketing plan further. Do not toy with yourself or just try to open in a certain space because you like the area. It is a simple yes or no answer. You have to make sure you have solid ground to stand on before you open so your business does not fail.

Associations and Clubs

Trade Associations

By definition, an association is an organization of people with a common purpose that has a formal structure. Associations connect people with a common purpose. Many states and cities have their own floral associations. Joining is a good way to get to know other florists or business owners who might not be in your direct area. They can send a client your way if they know someone who is visiting your area for a time, and you can do the same for them. You can meet people and swap information and tips you have learned. Joining a local association is a great way to interact with others in your trade.

Practical Pointer

Your regional Small Business Administration (SBA) holds a wealth of information. They have many wonderful programs like SCORE. The SBA's SCORE program helps link up retired business owners with newcomers. These retirees provide much information; participation often results in a unique mentorship and friendship as well.

Memberships

Become a member of anything and everything you can. Whether it is the local chamber of commerce or a floral club in your area, do what you can to make contacts and get your business recognized. You will also make friends and gain useful knowledge along the way. Do everything in your power to make meetings and help others. It will come back tenfold from other members who are willing to do the same in return.

Marketing Plan and Marketing Tools

The marketing plan is one of the most significant aspects of your business. This plan will create the image of your business that customers and potential customers will see. It helps shape your company and shows others what your business is all about.

A good marketing plan is well-rounded to include an image you would like to portray to your target customers, marketing materials you will use, and tactics such as sales, discounts, and promotions (where applicable).

Small businesses typically have different marketing plans than medium and large business. First, let us take a look at what you should include in your marketing plan.

Your small business plan should include:

- Customer demographics

- A description of competitors, including a SWOT analysis and the level of demand for the product or service

- A description of your business location, including advantages and disadvantages in terms of marketing

- A clear description of your products, services, and special features

- Your marketing budget, including all advertising and promotional costs and plans (if available)

❀   Pricing strategy

❀   Market segmentation

Your medium or large business plan should include:

❀   Executive summary

❀   Situational analysis

❀   SWOT analysis

❀   Objectives

❀   Strategy

❀   Action program

❀   Financial forecast

A large businesses marketing plan should be professionally made and include a title page, photos, and an appendix.

If you have never taken a business or marketing course, you probably will not understand some of these descriptions. Do not worry. They are broken down right here for you. Let us take a more detailed look at each of the business plan segments.

Small Business Plan Breakdown

Customer Demographics: Demographics are acquired data about a select population. The most commonly used demographics are race, religion, age, income, disabilities, mobility, education, home ownership, employment status, and location.

SWOT Analysis: A SWOT analysis is a planning tool that is used to evaluate Strengths, Weaknesses, Opportunities, and Threats. SWOTs can be as simple as drawing up a comprehensive list of these denominators or it can be an in-depth analysis of internal and external factors, too.

Level of Demand: The level of demand simply refers to how high the needs or wants are for your product in a particular area. For example, if there are already two flower shops in your ideal location, the level of demand will be low. On the other hand, if there are no flower shops in your ideal location, the level of demand will be high, which is ultimately what you want.

Description of Competitors: This is simply an analysis of your competition. It includes things like logo, services provided, products provided, and location. It is recommended to go in and shop your competition's products so you can get a better idea of what they are about. Mark your observations down in your description.

Description of Product, Service, and Features: This is a description of what you offer — what types of flowers your store will carry from day to day, extra services you provide like arrangement workshops, special features you offer like exotic hybrids, or a niche you provide for like weddings.

Marketing Budget: This is the allocated amount of money that you have dedicated toward your marketing plan for the entire year.

Pricing Strategy: The pricing strategy should detail where your marketing dollars are being spent. This section should include things like advertisements, promotions, decals, and logos.

Market Segmentation: This section is where you will put down where you feel you fit into the market after all of your research is complete. It should include a mixture of products, services, given prices, distribution methods, and ways you plan on promoting your business. Consistently improving in this area will help improve overall effectiveness.

Medium and Large Business Plan Breakdown

Executive Summary: In the most basic sense, an executive summary is an abstract. It is a smaller report within a larger report that gives the reader a sense of what is to come later in your marketing plan.

Situational Analysis: The size of the business will depend on the size of this section in your marketing plan. Most large businesses break this analysis into an external sector that includes economy, legal, government, technology, sociocultural, and supply chain subsections. The internal section often includes company resources (financial, people, time, and skills) and objectives like the mission statement, corporate objectives, financial objectives, marketing objectives, a description of the basic business philosophy, and long and short term objectives. Next, a market analysis is usually done that includes a market definition, market size, market segmentation, industry structure, competition and market share, SWOT analysis of competition, and market trends. Finally, a consumer analysis can be done that includes buying decisions, participants, demographics, psychographics, buyer motivation, buyer expectations, and buyer loyalty. Even if your business is not large enough to encompass such a section in the marketing plan, it never hurts to brief yourself on these subsections since they give you a closer look at your customers, employees, and business standings.

Objectives: Objectives can be any type of long or short term goals set for the company.

Strategy: The strategy section should first have a part that explains the methodology of research. It should also map up the product, customer segment, geographical marketing, distribution channel, and pricing methods.

Action Program: The action program, or implementation, helps keep the ball rolling. It should detail employee requirements, financial requirements, management information systems requirements, monthly agendas while monitoring results, adjustment mechanisms, and possible contingencies.

Financial Forecast: The financial forecast is just that — a prediction as to where the company is heading in the future. It should include a current financial summary, projections, assumptions, break even analysis, prediction of future scenarios, and a plan of action for each scenario.

Although it seems like quite a bit of labor to complete a marketing plan, having a working plan will help you see where you are spending unnecessary dollars, where you can swoop into a new market, where your competition is lacking, and where your own company could use a boost. Once it is written, yearly maintenance is all that is necessary for most businesses.

Next is choosing the image you want to project to your customers. You should make sure it goes with the atmosphere you want to create in the store for your customers. It would be silly to have a country basket with apples in a store that is downtown and funky. Make sure the ambiance of your physical business makes its way onto all other marketing materials. It will help the atmosphere and your good service stay on customers' minds long after they have left the store. Pick a logo or a key phrase that you put on signage, business cards, flyers, and any other materials that are placed in public. Have a mission statement and post it proudly on a Web site or in the store for all customers to see.

In Short: Logos are often an essential for a business. Your logo speaks volumes about you and is a symbol your customers will get to know and trust. The long term benefits of having the right logo will be incredibly advantageous for your business.

Once you have established your image, you can move on to other marketing materials. You should automatically opt for a sign on the facade of your store. Make sure it lights up; this way, even if the store is closed, the sign is still drawing attention to the shop. Make a marketing budget and stick to it. Choose carefully what you would like to do, whether it is brochures, press releases, flyers, business cards, mailers, e-mails, commercials, or newspaper advertisements. When you have chosen your marketing route, be sure to be repetitive and consistent. If you have chosen to use the local paper for advertising, pick a day or two to advertise consistently every week. If you are sending out weekly e-mails to customers, make sure they go out on the same day, at the same time each week. There is a rule in marketing: It takes customers five times to see an image before they recognize it, five more until they become interested, and another five times until they are willing to seek you out. This is why being repetitious and timely is so important; do not waste good marketing with irregularity.

Let us look more closely at some marketing tools.

Business Cards: These are a necessity. You can hand them out everywhere you go. Make sure you do not leave a room until everyone has one of your business cards in-hand. Put your chosen logo or slogan on it. Make sure there is plenty of contact information such as a street address, phone number, and e-mail address. You can also add simple directions to the store for a finishing touch.

Mailers: Mailers are much like flyers, only you send them via the postal service. You can opt to pick a target market, such as a specific neighborhood, or you can walk from box to box and put them inside. Do not stick them on car windshields or inside doors, as these options might appear tacky to some potential clients.

E-mails: E-mails are free and convenient. You can send them out in mass or just to a few people. Either way, they are a great marketing tool that is easy to use and, best of all, that will not dip into your budget.

If you decide to use a promotional e-mail, make sure it is clear who the e-mail is from, what it is about (use the subject line here), and includes return contact information and opt out information. You can include pictures but the bulk of the e-mail should be clear and to the point, almost purely informational.

❧ Sample E-mail ❧

Subject: Celebrate Easter with Atlantic Florist Charity Tea Party 2008

From: Stephanie, Owner, Atlantic Florist

Reply: steph@atlantic-florist.com

Date: March 21, 2008

This message has been sent by the owner of Atlantic Florist.

Dearest Valued Friend,

The time has come for Atlantic Florist's annually Charity Tea Party. As you might re-member, we will be providing tea, cookies, and holiday related activities at our store over the weekend before Easter. 100 percent of the proceeds from bouquets bought during this period will be given to St. Jude's Children's Hospital to buy Easter baskets for the children. We hope to see you here!

Sincerely,

Stephanie and the Staff at Atlantic Florist

Your e-mail address has not been given to any third parties. You have received this e-mail because you have requested it. If you do not wish to be contacted any longer via e-mail, please click here to opt out.

Atlantic Florist, 123 High Street, Flowertown, FL 55555

For additional information, please call us at: 555-123-5555.

Upon receipt, many customers will simply click an e-mail away as spam if they do not recognize who it is from almost immediately. Here are a few tips to avoid your e-mails being filtered or sent instantaneously to spam folders.

1. Send legit e-mails. Make sure it is clear who the e-mail is from and what it is about so that the customer will want to open it. Send only relevant information that involves the customer like promotions, sales, or important events.

2. Send out your e-mails in batches or slow your send speed. Although it may be more time consuming and the last thing that you want to do on a busy day, most spam filters will detect bulk e-mails immediately and try to bring them down. You can send your e-mails out in small groups or slow down your sending speed.

3. Get on the whitelist. The blacklist is a list of spammers, while the whitelist is accepted senders. Write to postmaster@domaintroublesendingto.com, explain your business and request a spot on the whitelist. You can also ask customers to add your e-mail address to their personal address book to avoid confusion.

4. Send directly to the recipient. Most people will delete an e-mail if it was not sent with their name on it. Since it is a floral business, you will be able to easily acquire a name to attach to the e-mail address. Make it more personal and your customers will be more than willing to read your updates.

5. Do not get tricky. It may seem like logic to try to trick the spam filters but it is not worth the effort. Follow the steps above and you will avoid them the right way.

Flyers: Flyers are so easy to print out that you can do it from home. For a more professional look, go to a copy store and ask for help with the layout and printing options. Use both sides of the paper. Put contact and other important information on one side. Put photos or a unique spin, such as a discount or seminar you are hosting, on the other. Place them at any location that will allow your frequent customers and potential new customers to see them, like your local supermarket.

Your flyer can be as simple as this, making it easy to print and distribute yourself as a money saver:

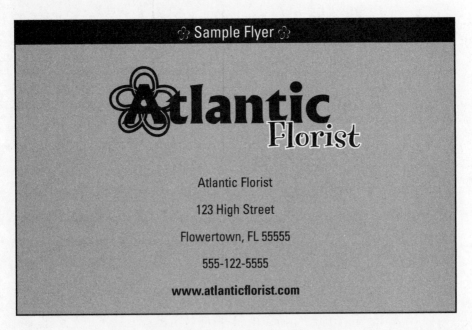

Make sure when you do your flyer the colors are cohesive, run parallel to your theme, and the entire thing stands out among other flyers and is attractive to the eye.

Press Releases: These are so easy that you can also do them from home. Research some press releases online and then format one from home in a Word document. Look up newspapers in your area and e-mail editors at these papers with an attachment of your press release. If they pick it up, it might appear in the paper for free. If you are lucky, the paper might even choose to cover your event in a featured article or in a special section.

Brochures: If your budget allows for them, brochures are a great way to connect with potential customers. Not only do they allow room for contact information, but they can show your creative side with photos of arrangements, your shop décor, or a picture of your friendly, smiling staff.

Paid Advertisements: Commercials, whether on television or on the radio, are often costly. Make sure you have the budget and that you do the proper research before taking this route. For example, rather than running your ad during a children's show, run it at a later hour when children are asleep and parents are the ones watching television. Although expensive, paid advertisements will often turn out to be worth your while if you use them strategically.

The easiest way to get your feet wet in the world of advertising is to up your ante in the local Yellow Pages. For additional fees, the Yellow Pages also offers priority placement, online business video profiles, and YPclicks!, which offers search engine marketing and YP Web solutions.

No matter which forum you choose, make sure your paid advertisement includes the who, what, when, where, and why of your business. A good sample Yellow Page ad might read as follows:

You will also want to include your logo so consumers begin connecting it with the store they drive or walk past. Also, make sure your phone number is clearly visible in any visual advertisement.

Free Publicity: Yes, it is as good as it sounds. Free media coverage is easier than most people first assume. Television stations, newspapers, and radio stations are always looking for new stories. Help them out by making suggestions. The best way to go about it is to make your store as newsworthy as possible. Make a list of accomplishments and other noteworthy things that your store has recently achieved or things that are in the works, like a charity event. Whenever you do something important for the community and your customers, let the media know. You might be surprised at how quickly they respond.

- Monthly charity events

- Flower arranging classes

- Wedding consultations

- Do regular arrangements for the mayor of Flowertown's galas

- Provide arrangements for the Flowertown Hotel

The best way to get noticed is to do a press release announcing your news. Choose one of the items on your list to focus on. Make sure it is professionally done on company letterhead and contains event specific information only. The last thing a journalist will want to do is sift through or read five pages to get to your main point. Make your press releases short and snappy. Always include your contact information, as well as the best times to reach you, and the date of your event. Draw up a list of media outlets and start faxing as soon as possible.

To make sure your press release is exciting enough to cover follow these tips:

- Make sure it is newsworthy. You may be excited about your new wedding contact, but will the entire town be excited? Put an interesting spin on it like "Celebrating our 100th contract wedding" to make it more newsworthy.

- Always make sure who, what, where, when, why, and how are covered.

⊛ A press release should never read like an advertisement for your store. If it does, it will be tossed aside. Make sure there are hard facts about you, your business, and the story you are covering.

⊛ Give yourself a hard minimum and maximum. A good rule of thumb is that 500 words is enough to give good information but not go overboard. A minimum of about 250 is just enough to cover the basics but try not to go much lower than that or your press release will presumably be lackluster.

⊛ Include contact information so that reporters can get in touch with you easily. The last thing you want is to miss a free front page story because you missed a phone call.

Here is a generalized press release template that is easy to follow and covers all the bases.

❀ Sample Flyer ❀

Atlantic Florist

123 High Street

Flowertown, FL 55555

555-123-5555

February 22, 2008

FOR IMMEDIATE RELEASE

*If the story is not available for immediate release you can choose to put "Embargoed until" and the available date instead.

Atlantic Florist is pleased to announce the first of many charity events at our store.

Our staff is putting together a workshop for those looking to learn the art of floral

❀ Sample Flyer ❀

arranging. The workshop will include one-on-one time with staff members. Flowers and tools will be provided and all proceeds will be donated to our chosen charity, The American Lung Cancer Society.

The workshop will run all day on Saturday, March 15, 2008, beginning at 8:00 a.m. to 4:00 p.m. A pasta dinner for participants and the community will begin at 5:00 p.m. right here in our store at 123 High Street. All are more than welcome.

Members of the media are invited to witness the workshop, donate to our chosen charity, and to enjoy delicious pasta with the rest of the community at the Pasta Party.

For more information, please contact:

Sandy Vogt, Head Florist

Atlantic Florist

555-123-5555 x2

There are many online tools that florists often do not use to their full advantage. Get a Web site up. You can build your own Web site on Internet provider sites like Google and Yahoo! or with a do-it-yourself type program such as **Web.com**'s Web Builder. To own full rights, make sure you register your domain name with a company that sells domains, such as **GoDaddy.com** or **Register.com**.

It can be anything from a simple page with contact information to a page done by a hired professional. Your Web site should reflect your creative image and be clean and neat. No matter how it is done, it does not hurt to get your name out onto the Web. You can also offer a newsletter and coupons through e-mail to customers who click on your site. You can write blog posts informing clients of goings on in the store or have a section featuring special offers. Blogs are also a great way to get in touch and talk flowers with your clients.

To help further attract customers, it never hurts to offer discounts or coupons where applicable. You can shape these to suit your fancy. Customers loyal to one florist might give you a go if they can get $5 off of their next bouquet or arrangement. Offer holiday and seasonal coupons on a regular basis. Discounts on supplies and other clearance items are also a great idea to get people in the door. Advertised sales always attract customers.

Florists also have an additional option to connect their Web site with FTDs. FTD has wonderful Affiliate Marketing Services that does all the work for you. The only downfall is they take a large chunk of change from the sales generated.

If you want to do the marketing yourself, you can put your Web site on many other Web sites for free. For instance, **Facebook.com** and **Kudzu.com** offer free services and are known to generate a lot of traffic.

Down to Business

Types of Ownership

Before you even consider any other business plans, you have to choose the type of ownership you would like to establish. It is absolutely imperative because the type of ownership you choose will ultimately affect every other decision you make. Not every type will suit you, so you should choose the one that best meets your business needs.

Sole Proprietorship

A sole proprietorship is the easiest of the choices. It is a one-man operation that is not registered with the state.

The upside is its simplicity. Many freelance florists are considered a sole proprietorship since it does not involve any fuss or paperwork. All you have to do is snap your fingers and say, "I am a business owner" and you really are. However, to make it legit you may have to follow permit laws, acquire a business license, and obey local tax registration regulations.

The downside is you are completely responsible for any liability that might come your way, including lawsuits and debt. That means a creditor can take your house if needed to pay off business debt, so you have to handle a sole proprietorship with care.

According to the state, a sole proprietorship is not legally separate from the owner. That means the law considers you and your business to be the same entity. Therefore, you will file your business income and loss on your individual tax return (IRS 1040). You will also be held responsible to withhold, as well as pay, your own income taxes quarterly. Usually an employer would do this for you; however, it is not as difficult as it seems. As a rule of thumb, you should simply withhold 30 percent of all earnings for your taxes. If done correctly, you should have no problems.

If you do decide to go all the way and register, generally sole proprietorships need only complete the all-purpose registration requirements. You will have to pay at least minimal taxes, but in turn you will receive your business license or tax registration certificate. You may also have to get an employer identification number from the IRS if you have employees.

Partnership

A partnership is nothing more than a business with more than one owner that has not registered with the state. This is then split into two sectors: general partnerships and limited partnerships. These can both be sealed with a simple handshake.

A general partnership is straightforward and the least expensive to maintain. A limited partnership usually consists of one partner who controls daily activity and is liable for debts while the other partners are restricted in their activities. These "silent" partners may invest but have little say in daily operations.

For any partnership, all partners are bound to the business in a personal manner, meaning that a creditor can legally lay siege on personal property if there are unresolved debts. How deeply each partner is involved should be drawn up in an agreement. The agreement should include if there is joint authority, joint liability, and taxes. It will help structure the partnership so that everything is agreed upon before the start of business. Every state has laws that govern partnerships and any going into one should be sure to follow these rules and consider them when drawing up an agreement.

A typical agreement should include the following:

- Name of the partnership

- Contributions

- Allocation of profits, losses, and draws

- Partner's authority

- Partner's decision making ability

- Management duties

- Adding new partners

⊛   Withdrawal or death of a partner

⊛   Dispute resolution

The big disadvantage of a partnership is that if one partner leaves, the entire company can fold. To avoid conflict at the end, partners can create a buyout agreement, which can be a subsection of the partnership agreement. It should explain what happens if a partner retires, passes on, becomes disabled, or leaves the partnership. This agreement will help the business continue on with little disruption.

Similarly to the sole proprietorship, you do not have to register with the state although you are solely responsibility for all taxes, debts, and liabilities that can come your way. The partnership registration process is almost identical to that of a sole proprietorship, too.

Corporation

To form a corporation, use the following checklist to complete the steps necessary before you can even open your doors:

⊛   Choose a name

⊛   Appoint directors

⊛   File articles of incorporation

⊛   Draft bylaws

⊛   Create an owner buyout agreement

- ❀   Hold a board meeting

- ❀   Issue stock

- ❀   Obtain necessary licenses and permits

- ❀   Retain your corporate status

When it comes to choosing a corporate name, under no circumstance can it be the same as another corporation on file. It must comply with state regulations such as ending with Corp., Inc., or Ltd., and it cannot continue government related words like bank or federal. There is no lengthy registration process. Once you file your articles of incorporation, the name is yours — assuming you have done the research and it is available.

Next up are your directors. These must be trustworthy individuals since they will make all the major policy and financial decisions for the corporation. You can also appoint yourself as a director, and most states allow a corporation to have only one director if there is only one owner. To start, this may be a logical way to go since you cannot trust anyone more than yourself when it comes to your business.

After you have picked a suitable name and appointed directors, you will need to file your articles of incorporation. This is traditionally done at the department or secretary of state's office in your state capital. These pages will merely create your corporation. They do not have to be very long and it usually only takes a few minutes to fill out the paperwork needed.

Once you are legally created, you will need to think about drafting corporate bylaws. These are the in-house regulations that govern daily operation. They should encompass the whole of the business. Traditionally, bylaws are inducted at the first board meeting.

Now is a good time to have the first meeting to negotiate:

- ❀ Fiscal or accounting year

- ❀ Appoint corporate offices

- ❀ Induct the bylaws

- ❀ Authorize the issuance of stock shares

- ❀ Implement an official stock certificate and corporate seal

It should be noted that you are not officially considered a corporation until you have deployed shares of stock because, by law, the division of ownership interest is a requirement for running a corporation and if you want the government protection that a corporation brings, you must follow these rules.

To issue stock, most corporations have to go through a set of hurdles that can become quite complex. They have to register with the Securities and Exchange Commission as well as the state security agency. It typically involves a lot of hours, legal man power, and lots of additional fees. Fortunately for small corporations, most are exempt from these strenuous registration activities.

As the owner of a corporation, you will be blessed with limited liability. This means you become separated in the eyes of the laws from your business. Therefore, if your business goes under, you do not necessarily have to personally because creditors do not have the right to seize personal property as a form of payment. However, you are completely responsible to keep exceptional records to maintain limited liability.

Now that you have issued stock and are formally a corporation, you must attain the proper licenses and permits before opening. This includes:

⊛   Employer Identification Number from the IRS

⊛   A state seller's permit

⊛   A business license

⊛   A tax registration certificate

⊛   A zoning permit

After obtaining all the right permits and licenses, your corporation is on the record and ready to go.

Business Plan

All store owners must have a business plan. This is a basic guideline of your business. It should be general enough that it will not need much tweaking over the years, but detailed enough that it covers any problems or issues that might arise. Your plan should include financial and accounting information, expenses, inflow, and all policies you plan on implementing. A business plan is often necessary when seeking out start up money for your business or when contributing to charitable causes.

When you are first starting out, do not overly complicate the business plan. Make it as simple as possible. In the most basic of terms, your business plan will be broken down into four main sections, including a description of your business, your marketing plan, your financial management plan, and your management plan. Supplemental items that should also be included are a cover sheet, an executive summary, supporting documents, financial projections, a statement of purpose, and table of contents.

Although it may seem a little bit daunting at first, broken down, it is not as difficult as it might seem.

Description of Your Business

On the surface it is a description of the business you plan to run. It is also much more than that. Your business plan should showcase how special your store is and what makes it stand out from others similar to it. State the obvious, like the fact you are going to operate a retail business. Top off simple facts like this with specific product types, types of arrangements you will sell, holiday events, or niche services you are going to provide. These items are like the icing on the cake to those reading your business description.

You will also want to provide a clear explanation of why your business will be more advanced than others and how you will bring in more revenue. You can also include minute details like store hours, changes in these hours during holidays, location, and the type of retail space you will be working in, along with reasons why it fits in with your stated business.

Conclude your description with short and long term goals and objectives. Make sure you support them with rationale and personal experience you have acquired in business. Do not skip over this part. It is crucial because it states exactly why you are starting the business, what you want it to be, and where you plan on taking it in the future.

Marketing Plan

Your marketing plan should always address the competition, pricing, advertising, and any public relations related items you plan on incorporating into your store.

The marketing plan is discussed in more thoroughly in Chapter 2: Marketing Research.

Financial Management Plan

Your financial management plan is the part of the business plan you will find yourself referring to repeatedly. It is certainly one of the most critical aspects to running a financially sound and successful business. This plan should clearly define how you want your money spent and should be as in depth as possible. As the years go on, you can tweak it as necessary. For example, the first year you may dedicate $2,000 to local advertisements in newspapers and $500 on Yellow Page ads. You might find that your Yellow Page ads are generating more business, so the next fiscal year you can tweak your financial management plan to increase the Yellow Page ad budget and decrease the amount spent on newspaper ads.

The financial plan should include your start up fees as well as operating fees. The start-up budget will focus on legal, professional, licenses, permits, equipment, insurance, supplies, advertising, promotions, accounting, utilities, and payroll — giving you a good idea of just how much capital it will take to open a fully functional business. Your operating budget at this point should feature the first six months of operation. After you are established, the start up budget will fall away and you can adjust your operating budget as needed.

This part of the plan should address the accounting and payroll systems, too. Many small business owners use the assistance of accounting software like QuickBooks while others opt for a human accountant. The first year, it is often wise to get a live accountant that can help you setup your financial management plan, accounting system, and payroll. Those who opt for software assistance can find fan favorite QuickBooks at **www.quickbooks.com**.

Management Plan

All businesses and employees need management. But who fills the management in on how to organize and control the store? The management plan does. This plan should include briefs on:

- ⊛   Your background and business experience and the reasons these items will benefit your business

- The names of management, even if you are the only employee

- Any assistance you plan on receiving (whether it is financial, consulting, or advice)

- All employee duties and responsibilities, including your own

- How hiring or firing employees will work

- A general summary of how the business will be run

Extras

To make your plan a professional one, be sure to include:

- A cover sheet with the name of your business, your own name, partners' names if applicable, address, phone number, e-mail address, other contact information, and a synopsis of the business plan

- A table of contents after the cover page

- A statement of purpose that summarizes your goals and objectives from now until the distant future

- An executive summary which should sum up the entire business plan — one to two lines on each section of the book

- Financial projections should be clear — include how much you need to start, how much you think you will earn, and reliable reasoning to back it up

⊛   All supporting documents, such as tax returns, a personal financial statement, or a copy of the lease or purchase agreement for your retail space

Before you embark on your writing journey, take a look at some resources that will help you better understand and detail your business plan. The Small Business Association (**www.sba.gov**) is full of articles and useful checklists, as is the Canada Business Service Center (**www.cbsc.org**). The Service Corps of Retired Executives (SCORE) is also a good resource. SCORE will link you with a volunteer who is willing to mentor you free of charge. The Web site, **www.score.org**, also has valuable articles and other information.

According to the Small Business Association (SBA) there are a few ways to ensure your business will hit the ground running with as little turbulence as possible. Here are a few suggestions:

⊛   Save as much money as possible before opening.

⊛   Understand how, if, and when you will begin making a profit.

⊛   Start small and grow with your profits.

⊛   Protect your personal assets.

⊛   Draw up a business plan.

⊛   Be competitive.

⊛   Put all agreements in writing no matter how big or small they are.

⊛ Have a goal to hire and retain the best employees.

⊛ Pay all of your bills as early as possible and always make sure your taxes are timely.

Financing

After you have decided to enter the floral world, have chosen your market, and have decided where you will situate yourself, you are ready to look at financing options. Financing can come from several different resources — the obvious, such as banks, partners, private investors, personal savings, and family and friends, or the lesser known, such as minority and women owner business assistance programs and the SBA. Carefully examine all the options that are potentially available to help you open your new business.

No matter which type of lender you choose, most will want you to sign off on a promissory note. In the most basic sense, it states, "You gave me $X so I promise to pay you $X plus X percent." Even if you shake on it with a family member or friend, you should still draw up a promissory note that defines the original amount, interest rate, and payment plan.

Helpful Hint   Documentation is the key if the IRS decides to audit your business.

Payment plans usually fall under one of four types — amortized, equal monthlies with a final balloon, interest only, or final balloon and single payments of principal and interest.

1. Amortized payments are typical of car loans and mortgages. Generally, the borrower pays the same amount for the duration of the loan. The payments are split between interest and principal balances. Once your payment plan runs out, the loan is fully amortized.

    A program like QuickBooks has an easy to use online calculator for this type of loan or you can ask your lender, or even local library, to print out an amortization schedule for you to follow.

2. Equal monthly payments are just that — equal monthly payments. Typically, you are mainly paying principal and then interest for a short time. Monthly amounts are usually lower than other loans; however, borrowers must always keep the big end balloon payment. The balloon is a large lump sum that pays off the loan in its entirety once the payment plan is coming to a close.

    Balloons also pose additional risks since they fluctuate throughout the length of the loan.

3. Interest only payments are paid out for nearly the entire lifetime of the loan. These payments do not get applied to principal so at the end of the loan, you will have to repay this entire amount in a single balloon payment.

4. A single payment of principal and interest does not require any payment plan. The borrower will simply pay back the entire loan at a specified date in the future. This is not usually offered at a commercial lender. It is a great way to draw up a promissory note with a friend or family member.

Lastly, read the fine print! Do not get duped with a penalty fee or an out-of-this-world waiver that takes away some of your legal rights.

Banks

Going to the bank and taking out a loan might seem like the most obvious choice, but it is not always the easiest route. Banks are wary of loaning money for retail start ups, especially to first timers due to high failure rates for these types of businesses. On the other hand, making a compelling argument why you want to do this and providing well-researched knowledge on the subject will make you more likely to succeed at a bank. The more serious you show them you are, the higher the chances become that they will give you the loan you want.

Banks often look for these requirements in a contender:

⊛ For those candidates with an existing business, a bank will usually want a means of cash flow that is adequate to make each loan payment.

⊛ For a new business, the bank will want to see a record of profitable ownership, operation in a similar business, or plenty of experience within the same business.

⊛   For any business, a bank will want the business owner to have an extensive financial reserve and plenty of personal collateral.

A friendly face is always a good starting point. Talk to someone at your personal bank whom you have worked with previously or are friendly with whenever you go in to complete a transaction. This person is a great jump-off point to ask loan questions or to request a meeting through. If you are turned down, try not to be too distraught. Often, the person you met with probably liked you, your passion, and your plan, but thinks the retail industry is too risky for the bank to become involved with your business. If you do score a meeting, be prepared. Bring a well-organized file or binder filled with documents that show other sources of financing you plan on using and other parts of your business plan. Always have backup resources. Even if the bank is willing to loan you something, it is not all you will need to open your business.

If you are thinking about using a bank, here are some more tips to help before you apply:

⊛   Build up your credit report. Work on getting unnecessary items off and high scores on.

⊛   Have a professionally done business plan ready.

⊛   Research and apply for the right type of loan.

⊛   Have specific purposes handy as to where the money is going and why.

Partnership

Bringing on a partner can be a good way to further your financing options. If you do not want anyone else interfering with your work, or you are not keen on sharing business ideas, a silent partner might be your best bet. A silent partner loans money, but has extremely little to do with daily business or decisions within the company. More often than not, they simply wait for their loan to be repaid or for the business to eventually go up for sale. Active partnerships can be split in many ways, too. A fifty-fifty partnering is often ideal for several reasons. Another partner might bring knowledge and skill that will be complimentary to yours. Having two people backing your business ideas will also be more appealing to potential investors.

Finding the right partner who will be an asset to your business is important. If you both want to be the head florist or the head honcho, you will most likely have problems. Conversely, if you can find a partner who understands that you are the head florist and he is coming in to incorporate his savvy management skills into the business, you might have found a perfect match. A new partner can also further expand your customer base by bringing a fresh crop of friends and family. It also means that, although you will both work hard, you can take a day off here or there or extend vacations, knowing that a trustworthy person is running the store.

Whether they are silent or active, be sure to select the best partner for you. Many relationships have been crushed due to a partnership gone sour. Make sure you are extremely compatible with whomever you choose and that they are not a close friend or family member in case something goes awry. If you approach everything with caution, are open and honest, and take the right legal measures, the partnership can be a winning one. You might also find a lifelong friend that you would not have had otherwise.

Private Investors

Private investors, although sometimes a bit nerve wracking, can be helpful when you are trying to fund your business. They are often more lenient than a bank. This is due in part to the fact you will be putting up collateral, typically the business itself, in case you cannot pay back your loan. If you are willing to put up this type of guarantee, seek out a reputable private investor. Most are mortgage brokers or private money lenders who know about business.

When you have found the investor you want to use, be prepared to answer several questions about the amount of money sought, the value of the property you are pledging as security (collateral), a detailed description of the property, and how you plan on using your funds. The lender will then lay out all the information you have given and assess the situation, focusing on the collateral. If the guarantee seems like a good one, a maximum loan amount that coincides with the amount of equity in the property up for collateral will be set. This equity provides a cushion for the investor, so if circumstances arise where you cannot pay on your loan, the investor will recoup his money by taking your property's equity.

Although private investors are often easier to get loans from than banks, many private investors find retail daunting, especially when dealing with perishables like flowers. Make sure that if you go this route, you find an investor who stands behind your ideas 100 percent and will not pull funds due to apprehension or to assist a larger business.

Small Business Association and Other Assistance Programs

Lesser-known ways to receive grants and monies can be found through minority and women business owner assistance programs or at your local SBA. The United States Department of Commerce offers help to minorities via the Minority Business Development Agency (MBDA). They have centers willing to extend a helping hand in the cities of Atlanta, Chicago, Dallas, New York, and San Francisco. Many states and individual cities and towns also have their own versions of the MBDA. Women business owners can also find an abundance of assistance through statewide programs. These resources offer valuable tools and financing options, but are rarely used to their full advantage. The SBA also has their branch of the Office of Women's Business Ownership Entrepreneurial Development. If these resources will not give you funding, they can at least furnish you with knowledge and point you in the right direction.

Personal Savings

Personal savings is another great alternative when you are looking for finances to support your business. Even though you do not want to deplete your personal savings unless it is absolutely necessary, using your own money has its advantages. You will not owe anyone a dime.

Having said that, be sure to set money aside for yourself, especially if your start-up capital came from your own piggy bank.

Family and Friends

A final choice to consider is family and friends. If you do decide to go this route, make sure you treat it like any other financing option you might encounter. Do not rely on a hearty handshake or try to jog your memory to remember who lent what amount. This can lead to disastrous results and guilt each time you see your family and friends. Make sure you write down details, sign them, and keep copies on file. Be exceptionally precise about how much you need, what it will go toward, and when and how you will repay your loan. Even if your business goes under, if you have taken the necessary steps, your family and friends should not be too upset; that is the risk they took when they lent you the money.

Accounting

Although you might not be a math whiz, you should certainly try to become more adept with numbers when it involves your business. Even if you hire an accountant, you should still understand the basics of your business' financials and how they relate to success.

Arming yourself with better financial knowledge can make or break your business, regardless of who you hire to handle your accounts. Take advantage of your local Small Business Development Center or community college. These learning centers often offer account or finance-related classes that can make a strong impact on your understanding of your financial situation. Do not sign up for advanced classes; start with the basics and work your way up. You will be proficient in no time.

To start, here is a basic accounting glossary of terms that every business owner should know:

- ❀ **Account:** Financial information clustered according to customer or purpose.

- ❀ **Accounting:** The general term for tracking your business' income and expenses to find your financial and tax status.

- ❀ **Accounts Payable:** Any amounts that your business owes others.

- ❀ **Accounts Receivable:** Any amounts that your business is expected to receive.

- ❀ **Bad Debt:** Money owed that cannot be collected at present.

- ❀ **Balance Sheet:** A statement that includes your business' assets, liabilities, net worth, and equity.

- ❀ **Bookkeeping:** This refers to the keeping of the date, source, and amount of all revenues and expenses.

- ❀ **Invoice:** A written record of transaction that requests payment.

❀ **Ledger:** The physical embodiment of bookkeeping. Your ledger will hold invaluable information like revenues, expenses, accounts receivable, and accounts payable. Today, ledgers are available in paper or electronic form.

❀ **Net Income:** Gross income expenses or, in simpler terms, your profit.

❀ **Statement:** A statement is a summary of invoices.

Methods

Broken down, there are two basic accounting methods, accrual and cash. The accrual method is often used in businesses where inventory is prominent, floral included. The cash method means you are recording an invoice as revenue when you send it and an expense when you receive a bill that your business is supposed to pay; this is the simplest method. All businesses must choose one way.

There are three fundamental statements to use with the chosen accounting method. The profit and loss statement, also known as the P & L, is setup monthly. It allows business owners to get a sense of where they stand each month. This is often setup in ledger style. The cash flow statement simply allows you to see how much is coming in and how much is going out. Finally, the balance sheet shows all of your business' assets versus its liabilities, or how much you own in comparison to what is owed. This statement is a good way to see whether you can increase your prices to make more, can afford a vehicle, need to cut costs anywhere, or should find new suppliers to help ease some of the pains of business. The balance sheet is a great way to see where your business can be cut back or can be allowed to grow and flourish.

Financial Cycles

Every business needs specific financial cycles. You will need to decide when your fiscal year will begin; this will all depend on your business setup. Sole proprietors should opt to coincide the calendar year with their fiscal year. Business income for a sole proprietorship is worked as a Schedule C on income tax, and Schedule C is always filed by the calendar year. On the other hand, corporations use a different tax configuration. It would be wise for a corporation to choose their fiscal year according the logic of how their business runs. For instance, most florists' busy time should correlate with the first quarter of their year. So if you are extremely busy during the winter holiday season, make that the first quarter and the second quarter will fall over another important holiday run that includes Easter.

Bookkeeping

Unless you are opening a floral mecca, daily bookkeeping should be simple. If you ask any business guru for a piece of advice, they will tell you to keep every receipt for even a penny spent on your business. Keep the receipts together in one spot and record them in your ledger weekly, if not daily, so that bookkeeping does not start to eat up hours of your days. Finally, use summaries in the form of a financial report so you can see your monthly profits and expenses with ease.

Checkbook

The checkbook will be imperative from the start of your business. No matter how big or small your business is, do not ever intermingle your personal checks with business ones. Open up a separate business account and get a checkbook and check card that coincide with that account alone. It will be much easier to keep tabs on what went where for bookkeeping and tracking purposes. It is also unprofessional to mix business with pleasure in such a manner. To add a professional flair, dub the account's name after your business so that printouts have your business name at the top.

Accounting Methods

There are many ways to keep track of your accounts in today's world. You can go old-fashioned with statements and checkbooks or use newer technology, like QuickBooks software. You can also hire an accountant or keep track through monthly profit and loss statements.

The Traditional Way

Tracking your finances the old-fashioned way, through a ledger notebook, is still an easy and smart way to be hands-on about your business' accounting. Keep it simple. Use one side for income and the other for expenses. You can pick up a ledger at any office supply store.

Choose a time, whether it be the end of each month, quarter, or year, and have a qualified accountant check over your ledger. They should review and balance them, let you know exactly what you have in your accounts, and give you some tips on how to keep better records of your finances.

Software

Today, software abounds. It is often incredibly user-friendly and makes accounting much easier. Having said that, you will still need to make sure time is spared to update your programs and enter information on a set, periodic basis. Try to choose a time slot, such as one hour each Friday morning, to do your bookkeeping.

There are several good programs available for use. Two of the most common are QuickBooks (**www.quickbooks.com**) and Microsoft Office (**office.microsoft.com**). Ask around to see what other business owners prefer and research to see what will work best for you. Make sure that when you do find the right product, you take the time to set it up properly and log in all the required information. This will save the headache of doing it later while you are trying to do your weekly or monthly bookkeeping.

It is also wise to logon to the program's Web site frequently to see if there are any updates. Signing up for e-mail or newsletters will let this information come to you, rather than you having to seek it out. Tax products are constantly upgraded due to ever-changing tax codes, so make sure you have updated information on your tax program.

Accountant

While your business is extremely small, doing your own bookkeeping is acceptable. Hiring an accountant can, however, easily make or break your business. Small business or retail accountants are often affordable and will help you save more than they charge. Your accountant will be the little push you might need to keep your information together and up-to-date. He will also help keep your records accurate and should be able to provide you with more knowledge on faster, easier accounting methods; this will make tax time a breeze. Building and growing your business can be easy if you have an accountant behind you. Gaining additional capital will also be much simpler. Knowing just how much you have in the bank will allow you to use special opportunities — such as sales, upgrading your workshop, or stocking more supplies — to your advantage. Most businesses that do not have an accountant do not have as accurate of records as they could, and they often miss out because they do not have time or want to re-create their records to figure out just what they have.

Deciding on an accountant is a big step. Call at least a dozen accountants and ask questions pertaining specifically to your business, such as, "What kind of small business experience do you have?" and "How familiar are you with retail, florists in particular?" You will also want to make sure that anyone you meet with is a tax accountant. There are so many specifications in tax law that it would be nearly impossible to run your business, keep your books, and learn all the tax rules. Asking smart questions will enable you to cross several names off the list. Setup meetings with accountants who sound promising. Face to face, you will be able to see who makes you feel more comfortable and will be able to provide you with the services you seek.

Income and Expenses

When you enter the world of retail business, have a good idea of where you are receiving income and what your expenses are. A high regard for knowing where your money is at all times, where it is coming from, and where it is going are exceptionally important values to keep throughout the longevity of your business.

Auto

All floral business should have a designated delivery vehicle. This vehicle should never be used for personal reasons, as this will make keeping detailed records of your business' means of transportation easier. Record everything from oil changes and gas to tune-ups. Using the Internal Revenue Service (IRS) mileage rate will make recording easier, rather than prorating expenses. Be sure to keep up with this because the IRS tends to change the rate annually. Keeping accurate records will make tax time much easier. It will also help you see how much you are spending on your vehicle and where you can cut costs since vehicles are often an expense that eats away at your budget.

Supplies

When buying supplies, you will want to make sure you take the most resourceful route possible. Long-term supplies, like a cooler, should be economical. Try to get energy efficient models that will help save money in the future. If you have to pay a little bit more now, do so. Do not buy something just because it is cheap. A cheaper model might cost you more during its lifetime due to leaks or inefficient cooling. Furthermore, nothing is better than having the proper tools handy in a time of need. Here is a basic equipment list to get you started:

- ❀ A large selection of fresh cut flowers

- ❀ A selection of flowering plants

- ❀ A selection of green foliage plants

- ❀ A selection of vases in a variety of forms (round, square, tall, short, globe, and slender) and materials (glass and plastic)

- ❀ A selection of lined baskets with handles

- ❀ A large selection of lined or plastic containers in a variety of forms (round, square, bowl, oblong, triangular, and other shapes) for arrangements

- ❀ A selection of buckets in various sizes

- ❀ A large supply of floral foam

- ❀ Several rolls of stem tape, floral tape, and ribbon

- ❀ A hot glue gun and aerosol glue

- ❀ Floral dyes and spray paints

- ❀ A variety of sharp knives, secateurs, and scissors

- ❀ A variety of stands, shelves, and other display equipment

- Coolers, preferably walk-in and stand alone

- Plant care equipment such as food and water

- Stationary for order taking and notes

- A cash register

- A debit or credit card machine

- A calculator

- A computer for online orders and e-mail replies

- A fax machines for faxed orders and fax replies

- A telephone

- Plenty of pens and pencils

- Several large garbage cans

In terms of flower supplies, try to maintain excellent relationships with your vendors and then use them to your advantage. Always keep a level head and professional presence, but also be friendly. Know that your vendors are trying to run a business too, so if they ask for a favor, kindly oblige. They will surely return your act of kindness at some point in your relationship. On the other hand, if an affiliation is not functioning the way you planned, weigh the pros and cons of continuing it and do not hesitate to cut ties if something is not working to your advantage, or you find you are giving more than receiving.

Please see the Flower Glossary, the Product, and Arranging sections to see larger lists of different flower supplies.

Employees

Employees are a hefty expense for retail businesses. Although it is difficult and tiring running a store on your own, paychecks, social security, workers' compensation, and other employee related expenses tend to add up quickly. If you do decide to take on an employee or two, make sure you are fair. Offer reasonable pay, good benefits, vacation time, and any other amenities you would want as an employee. If you are just, your employees will want to work hard when they are in the shop. Employees should pay for themselves in a relatively quick manner, or you might consider going back to a one-man operation.

Payments, Invoices, and Receipts

When you are figuring out how you want your clients to pay you, choose wisely. Many orders are taken over the phone and a good way to ensure payment is to allow a credit card option. Be sure you allow top names like Discover, Visa, MasterCard, and American Express. Most have a per-charge fee; even though American Express' rates are higher, it is a widely used card, so it should not be ruled out.

If you decide to allow checks, make sure you have an immediate verification service. On the other hand, most clients that have checks also have a debit card, which is much easier to use and will process immediately.

Collections

If you start to develop business clients that buy on a larger scale, you might want to consider offering accounts. Bigger businesses are often harder to obtain funds from than smaller clients, so make sure you setup a relationship that will ensure success on both ends. For starters, establish a payment period or turnaround time upfront. Whether it is weekly, monthly, or quarterly, make sure the payment period has a specified time and billing cycle. For example, if you bill clients biweekly, be certain you give them seven full days to pay the bill. Besides the billing, you will also want to institute a limit. Just because your client's business might be big, it does not mean they have endless means of wealth to pay you back. You will also want to have a list of approved users for each account. To make it even easier, insist that only one person, two at the most, be approved for the account so you are not constantly dealing with someone new.

Paying Yourself

Making sure you pay yourself for all of your efforts is essential. So many times, small business owners dump everything they have back into their business — physical labor, mental energy, and their money; all of it. For the first year or so, when you are just starting out, putting as much as you can back into your business is wise, and you should take note that funds will be tight until your customer base starts to grow. But after a few years, you will want to start paying yourself. Do not fall into the trap of giving but never receiving. This will lead to burnout and you and your business will suffer the consequences. Even if you decide not to give yourself a verified paycheck, at least take yourself or your family out to dinner or to a movie a few times a month so it is worthwhile. If a paycheck is imperative from the start, decide how big it needs to be. Pay yourself enough, but not so much that there is excess in your personal account but not in your business account.

Policies

Every business must establish policies. They can be concerning the store, employees, customers, deliveries, or anything else related to the business. Make sure once you instate a policy that you stick to it. Do not be lax about it or your set will fall apart. Rather, install policies that your business can only benefit from but are easy to follow so they do not become a burden.

Employee policy should always comply with federal and state law. It should be written in a way so that it is never out-of-date. If you have employees other than yourself, it is advisable to seek the expertise of a small business attorney who will make sure that your policy covers all the right bases. Here is a sample of what you can include in your own policy:

- ✸ **Core Values:** Clearly state what your company stands for, values, and expects.

- ✸ **Attendance:** Detail the consequences of lackluster attendance. Also include the acknowledgments that come with stellar attendance. This will help motivate employees.

- ❀ **Work Schedules:** Include the store hours and where the schedules are located in the back of your store.

- ❀ **Confidentiality:** Let your employees know how their confidential information is handled. Also make a point to show employees that personnel files are under lock and key.

- ❀ **Vacation Leave:** Provide an exact number of days, what they are allowed to be used for, and how an employee can get to them to take a vacation.

- ❀ **Sick Leave:** Again, provide an exact number of days.

- ❀ **Family and Medical Leave:** If applicable, lay out how long and the payment terms for a family or medical leave.

- ❀ **Drug/Alcohol Testing:** If you want your employees tested, make a point of when, where, and why so your employees get tested on time.

- ❀ **Drug/Alcohol Use:** Include what you feel fits into the drug and alcohol use mold and state disciplinary actions if anybody is caught using or coming in high or drunk to work.

- ❀ **Smoking:** Although it is not illegal, smoking can cause issues between employees. Designate a smoking area and include it in your policy.

- ❀ **E-mail and Computer Usage Policies:** Clearly state who is allowed to use the computer. Detail what those with access can and cannot look at. Because of the broad span of content today, it is smart to block all other sites except those that have contact with orders.

❀ **Dispute Resolution:** This section should have a clear cut answer for employees in a dispute. Lay out ground rules and let the employees know who they can come to for a one-on-one. From there, a group session should be considered to find a common solution for disgruntled employees. It should also include disciplinary actions.

❀ **Violence Resolution:** In today's crazy world, this part is imperative. Lay strict ground rules that forbid all violence. It simply should not be tolerated in the work place and those who participate should know that it is grounds for immediate termination.

❀ **Harassment:** This is another issue that should not be tolerated. State what is considered harassment and disciplinary actions that accompany it.

❀ **Insurability of Drivers:** This section should provide guidelines for all of your delivery drivers and their insurance. It should also state where your delivery vehicles are insured and policy details.

Remember, these are just suggestions. When it comes to employee policies, adopt them to suit your business. If it is only you, it would be silly to add in many sections like confidentiality. Conversely, you should still setup a brief policy that acknowledges items like vacation days and attendance.

You can also add a group of in-store policies. They can be anything you want to instill in your business. These policies can constitute anything having to do with your store, including but not limited to payment methods, deliveries, orders, product guarantees, and pricing. Hang these policies where all customers and employees alike can see them so there are no surprises. When you are implementing employee policies, create a list that is separate from your in-store policies. These policies can range from rules and regulations to customer service and anything in between. Hang this set in the break room or in a special place that employees see every day before their shift begins.

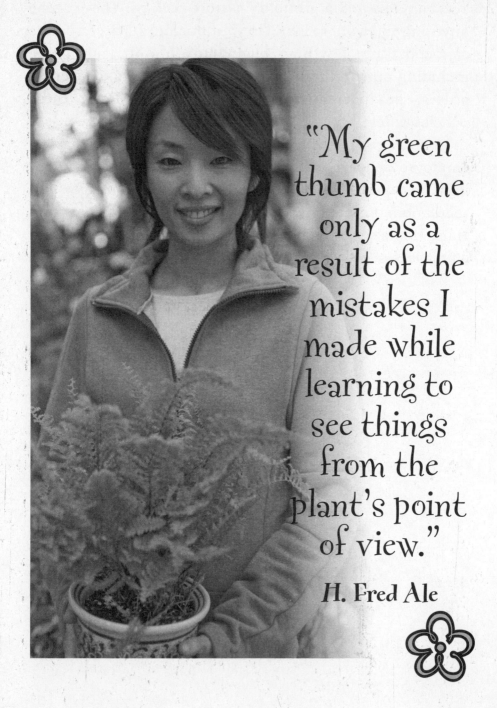

"My green thumb came only as a result of the mistakes I made while learning to see things from the plant's point of view."

H. Fred Ale

Legally Speaking

Every business needs to protect itself. Cover yourself from all sides because legal matters are serious in today's society and can cost the ultimate price — your business and reputation.

Insurance and Benefits

Insurance is the first step to covering your business. This includes insurances that cover anyone that walks through your door (liability), your physical location (property), and your employees (disability, worker's compensation, unemployment, and health). Find a qualified insurance broker to help you gather all the information and different insurances you and your business will need. Choose a broker by way of the methods discussed for accountants. Phone several, weed out the bad, and meet face-to-face with the good. An excellent broker will do his or her job to the fullest and will send notices of renewals or changes in policies. He or she will also offer different options and break everything down into understandable terms for you.

Liability

By definition, liability insurance coverage is compensation to third parties who are injured or whose property is damaged due to the fault of the insurance holder (you).

This is the most important insurance. Things happen that nobody can predict. Liability covers you if someone trips over a rug in your shop and breaks his arm. In today's world, people are quick to sue, no matter how long they have been a customer, even if it is no one's fault but their own. Lawyers will come at you from every possible angle: "Why was your rug there?", or "How could you have such a messy shop that someone would break their arm?" This happens even if nothing could have truly prevented the accident. You cannot stop people from suing you, but you can use liability insurance to protect your business from bankruptcy due to a lawsuit. If you operate out of your own home, make sure your zoning allows you to have a business first. If everything checks out, get a rider on your homeowner's policy that covers business practice or get a separate liability insurance policy.

A general liability policy will cover any damages that your business is ordered to pay to an individual who is injured on your property, whether ha customer, supplier, business associate, or an employee.

Product liability insurance will protect you from a lawsuit in which a customer claims the product you provided injured them. For example, if a customer claims that your flowers gave them a severe allergic reaction, your product liability policy will protect your business.

Lastly, auto liability insurance will cover any damage that you or an employee may inflict during a business related accident. If your business handles deliveries, you need auto insurance on your vehicle. It is legally required in Mississippi, New Hampshire, Tennessee, and Wisconsin, though it is never a bad idea to have coverage if you have a delivery vehicle, especially one that has your logo emblazoned on the side. Even though insurance for delivery vehicles often costs more, let your insurance agent know you are using it for your business and not for personal reasons. Pay all additional costs you may incur and do not try to skimp. The worst thing that could happen is you get in an accident and do not have the proper coverage to take care of the damages. This can certainly put a dark cloud over your business, especially if the local paper features the accident in a write-up the next day with your business' name splashed across the side of your delivery vehicle.

Property

This type of insurance will cover any damage or loss to your business' property. A good policy will cover:

- ⊛ Fixtures, like lighting or carpet

- ⊛ Equipment and machinery

- ⊛ Office furniture

- ⊛ Computers and other electronics

- ⊛ Inventory and supplies

- ⊛ Personal property kept at the business

After you establish what will be covered under the policy, you will have to research what types of losses will be covered. The majority of commercial property insurance policies come in the forms of basic, broad, or special coverage. A basic policy will cover things out of your control like a fire, explosion, storm, smoke, or a sprinkler leak. A broad policy will cover hefty damage like structural problems or water damage. Finally, the special coverage will provide a more extensive form of protection and will cover everything under the sun, including theft. Premiums will be high but if your business is in a high risk area, it may be worth it.

Before you buy a property policy, or any policy for that matter, read all the fine lines. Make sure you understand what you are reading, too. You should be able to distinguish the coverage limits, deductibles, copayments, and how the company repays a claim with ease. If you do not fully understand something, be sure to ask. And if your business is home based, you might want to check on how your homeowner's insurance policy will need an upgrade.

Disability

Accidents you may never have dreamed of in a million years can happen. Any savvy business owner should have disability insurance. This will cover you in case something happens and you can no longer perform your job at a satisfactory level, if at all.

There are two kinds of disability insurance, short-term and long-term. Short-term will cover you immediately. Short-term is often expensive. Long-term is cheaper, but does not kick in for several months — six months for most policies. If you want to save and opt to invest in long-term disability only, make sure you have yourself covered for the six months before the insurance kicks in. Try to save a few months pay in an emergency account so you would be covered if something were to happen.

Also, take note that most disability policies will not cover the full amount you were making previously, so you will have to be able to recoup costs in other ways. It is always smart to have a backup plan before anything happens.

Worker's Compensation

Worker's compensation is another insurance small business owner's often take for granted and pay minimally on. Considering the definition of worker's compensation — a program that provides replacement income and medical expenses to employees who are injured or become ill due to their jobs — you should not skimp here either. Although it might be painful making payments when none of your employees are injured, should one become injured or ill, these benefits can extend to dependents or survivors if your employee is killed on the job, which can be expensive. However, if an employee quits, was laid off, or was terminated, they are no longer eligible for these rights.

Always be thoughtful of those who work for you because if the injury or illness is bad enough, and they can claim you were at fault, employees can completely bypass worker's compensation and sue for damages that can include punitive, pain and suffering, and also mental anguish. If you do not have worker's compensation available or you ask an employee not to make a claim, they can report you and you will more than likely lose your business. So, paying for worker's compensation is a great idea.

Unemployment

Unemployment benefits will pay employees a certain percentage of their typical wage for up to 26 weeks, and in rare cases an additional 13 to 20 weeks on top of that. Let us take a peek at different scenarios surrounding these benefits.

"I quit!": Employees that resign on their own can only qualify if they left for good reasons, which include personal reasons like a spouse's relocation or an injury that you can no longer perform your job with. An easier explanation: if they quit, nine times out of 10 they will not be able to receive unemployment benefits. Since it is administered by the state, and not the employer, unemployment regulations vary from state to state. Check with your State Labor Department to make sure you are upholding the law.

"I got laid off!": If you find it necessary to cut back on staff for any reasons, chances are, all employees that are cut loose will be collecting unemployment shortly after.

"I got fired!": The same rules apply for employees that were fired due to financial reasons or staff cutbacks.

However, if they were terminated due to poor performance or misconduct, unemployment will not be granted.

In most cases, staffers will have to go through the typical unemployment compensation system, which varies in each state. They will typically file through steps similar to these:

1. **Filing a Claim:** They will file with their state and will receive a written notice shortly after.

2. **Determination of Eligibility:** The state will decide whether or not your former staffer can collect unemployment benefits.

3. **Hearing:** If the employee disagrees with the government's actions on his claim, he has the right to appeal. The appeal will lead to a hearing in front of a state appointed hearing officer. Here, the employer and employee are both allowed to give evidence in front of a lawyer and witness.

4. **Administrative Appeal:** If your ex-employee disagrees with the hearing office's final decision, he can take the next step and appeal it to a governmental agency for review. This review will be based only on the previous hearings documentation.

5. **Judicial Appeal:** And if he still does not hear what he wants to hear, your former employee can take it to the top and into the state court system. This is a rare occurrence.

Health

Illness can happen quickly, and a severe illness and prolonged hospital stay can wipe out your funds and put you out of business. Sadly, many small businesses skimp on their health care and lose out in the end. Do not fall into this health insurance trap. Research and call around. Some health insurance policies are astronomical, but if you speak with several companies, you can often find one that will work within your means. Once you have basic health insurance, you might want to consider adding dental and eye care to round out your employee's health benefits. A happy, healthy employee is more productive than an ill one on unemployment.

Although it can be confusing, the first step to choosing the right health care plan is to understand the basics of how the system works. To start, you should know that most plans are classified as "fee for service" or as "managed" care. There are several differences between the two. Let us take a look at the difference between the two.

Fee for Service: Fee for service plans, also known as "indemnity plans," are sold by insurance companies. Employees are allowed to visit any doctor and referrals for specific doctors or specialists are unnecessary. They also cover nearly all medical conditions that may arise. As an added bonus, most fee for service plan providers will directly bill your insurance company. However, there are still some providers floating around that will require you to file a claim with your insurance company to compensate your money the old-fashioned way.

What will I pay with a fee for service plan?

- ❀ You will still need to pay premiums, which is the fee that to take part in the provider's plan. You can opt to deduct the premium costs right from your employee's checks. As a sign of good faith, some employer's help pay some of their employees premium costs, even if not required to.

- ❀ You will also need to pay deductibles, which is the out-of-pocket amount before the plan kicks in. Insurance companies offer many options, but keep in mind that the higher the deductible, the lower your premium.

- ❀ Lastly, you will have to pay coinsurance. Once the deductible is met, most providers will pay a percentage of the remaining cost, but will also want you to put in for the rest.

Managed Care: Managed care plans use what they call "networks." These networks are comprised of contracted doctors, hospitals, clinics, and other health care providers. Most of the time, this means your employees will need to use a participating health care provider; however, some companies will pay for any provider but will offer incentives to use their chosen ones. They also only pay for services that are "medically necessary" and have a specified list of drugs that they cover. The counter to this is that managed care plans are often significantly more affordable than fee for service plans. These plans also encourage preventative care to avoid costly medical treatment in the future.

Managed care plans fall into three categories: health maintenance organization (HMO), HMOs with point of service (POS), or preferred provider organization (PPO).

⊕ **HMOs:** These plans require you use specific providers within the HMO network. Here you will choose a primary care physician. This physician is typically in charge of all of your medical care and will need to provide referrals if you are looking to see another provider or specialist.

⊕ **POS:** Here you may use non-network providers without a physician's referral. The downside is you will have to pay more money to use these out of network providers. The POS plan is often just an add-on to an HMO plan and requires an additional fee.

⊕ **PPO:** With this plan you are free to see whichever provider you choose and you do not need to choose a primary care physician. The hidden agenda here is that you will pay less if you use providers within the network.

What will I pay with a managed care plan?

⊕ Premiums

⊕ Deductibles

⊕ Coinsurance

⊕ Copay: Copays are the sum you will have to pay every time you make a trip to a provider or order a prescription. Most plans will have you pay a certain amount over the course of one year. Once that total is reached, they will pay 100 percent of copay costs for the remainder of the year.

Finding and Purchasing Insurance

The easiest way to make sure you have yourself covered is to hire an insurance broker. Insurance brokers make it their business to break down polices and get you the best deal they can. On the same note, many insurance brokers are paid on commission and will try to sell you anything to the point you might be over-covered, not to mention overpaying. Find one that is reputable or one not paid by commission.

When you find somebody you like, make sure they understand your business, the activities you conduct, and the potential risks. Surprisingly, you may be able to find a broker who specializes in flower shops and has as unique package policy deal, tailored specifically for those in the industry. A broker who is in your corner will be able to guide to the right policies and premiums while an average broker may get you covered, but with sky high premiums and the wrong coverage.

When running a business with employees, you will have to seriously consider the previously mentioned worker's compensation, unemployment, and disability. These are largely state regulated, so research and follow the rules or you can run the risk of a multimillion dollar lawsuit.

Legal Issues

Legal issues are not always a bad thing, and every business has to deal with them. When you chose the way you structured your business and opted for a specific auto insurance policy, legalities were there. Make sure you know the basics on these legal matters.

Corporate Configuration

The way that you configured your business plays a huge role in the way legal matters will be handled and resolved, should they arise. If you chose to be a sole proprietorship due to the simple nature of the structure, you also put your personal belongings at risk. Corporations, although incredibly detailed and complicated, protect you the most, but are also a more costly way to do business. Partnerships are in the middle. Before you decide which way you want to structure your business, lay it all out and see what you are willing to risk if any legal issues should arise. Please see more on this issue in Chapter 3: Down to Business.

Service Contracts

Most regularly operating floral businesses will not need service contracts. On the other hand, if you are a niche business, like a wedding florist or a landscaper, you will need the right service contracts to keep you covered. This contract will make it completely unmistakable what the exact services you are providing will be, what you expect from your clients, what your client pays for, the part of the deal you will provide in terms of funding or supplies, when payments are expected, and the consequences of a broken contract. All service contracts should consist of your fee structure and can also include a limited liability statement and warranty of your services. Address some common potential legal matters in your contract so that clients know what to expect upfront. For example, if a client purchases flowers for a church fundraiser and they all die before the event begins, who is liable? Your best bet to ensure your contract does not have loopholes is to hire a lawyer to write a basic contract you can change on an as-needed basis.

Employees

To keep your business structure as simplistic as possible, hold off on hiring employees as long as possible. Employees will make your situation complicated. Yet, to truly grow a business, having skilled employees is a necessity. They ease your workload and can allow you time to concentrate on your favorite aspects of the business.

Employee Alternatives

Rather than hiring employees right away, start off by outsourcing as many business objectives as possible. For example, you cannot run a store and deliver orders during a busy season. Hire an outside delivery service you can use on an as-needed basis to avoid the complications of hiring employees. Better yet, hire a subcontractor or freelancer. These people are self-employed and will work job-by-job, or on an as-needed basis.

The top 10 tips for avoiding legal trouble with your employees are:

1. Treat your workers with the same respect you would like them to give you in return.

2. Communicate effectively.

3. Be consistent.

4. Give evaluations regularly.

Helpful Hint

5. Make all decisions based on business relations.

6. Do not punish the messenger.

7. Implement sound polices and follow through with them.

8. Be a good record keeper.

9. Take action when necessary.

10. Be tactful.

Privacy

As much as snooping and juicy gossip is a part of our nature, it is also illegal in many circumstances. As a boss, it is your job to ensure that each employee is guaranteed his or her privacy.

There are many ways that privacy can be invaded. Whether it is a situation that concerns you directly or is one occurring between two employees, the sharing of private matters not meant for the ears of others can wreak havoc on your business, not to mention the ways it can interfere with employee's personal lives. Here are a few legally recognized examples of invasion of privacy you should try to avoid:

⊛ **False Light:** Much like the name states, this is when

someone is portrayed in a highly offensive manner unjustly. For example, an employee is accused of stealing arrangements, when in reality it is the UPS man sneaking in and doing the dirty deed.

❀ **Disclosure of Private Facts:** This occurs when private or embarrassing information about an individual are put on public display without a legitimate public concern. This is usually a case of gossip gone bad, but it can take a toll on an employee mentally if unwarranted information about him or her is leaked.

❀ **Intrusion:** Intrusion takes place when a person has a realistic reason for privacy that is completely obliterated by someone else. A perfect example is eavesdropping on personal phone calls.

Although these types of invasions of privacy will not completely be avoided, it is important to stake a claim and let your employees know where you stand in the matter.

To legally bind your stance on privacy and protect yourself, you can have your employees or any other person entering your building daily (think mail carrier), sign noncompete and confidentiality agreements. Both agreements cover your business and all of your insider secrets that employees might otherwise jeopardize.

A confidentiality agreement is essential if you often hire freelancers. This agreement forbids them to share any information they have learned at or about your business with other employers. A noncompete agreement states that an employee cannot start-up their future business in your locale and try to take your clients based on previous knowledge and access to the client base they had. Although it might be unnecessary to have freelancers sign a noncompete, you can add a line to their confidentiality contract that states your client base belongs to your business and your business alone.

In reality, you cannot stop former employees from trying to take your customer base, but if you have these forms signed, you do have their signature showing that they previously agreed not do this. You can decide from there whether legal action is necessary.

On that note, all employees are not out to get you. Most plan on opening in a market where there is little or no competition from an established business. They are simply there to learn and then move on. Do not be paranoid or too strict about these agreements. If employees refuse to sign these agreements, they probably had other intentions.

Worker's Compensation

Worker's compensation can be found under both federal and state law. If you plan on having any employees, this is absolutely necessary. This compensation covers employees in any instance of job-related injuries. If you do not want to pay for injuries and paychecks out of your own pocket, you should look into having worker's compensation insurance for your employees.

Vacation and Medical Leaves

Although it may hit your company hard, it is in your best interest as an employer to provide for your employees. This includes vacation time and any form of medical leave.

Surprisingly, offering sick and vacation time is not required by the government. Happy employees are often profitable ones. Conversely, you do not have to go overboard when offering additional benefits. Simply provide a policy that is attractive to employees, but still makes sense financially for your business.

If you would like to provide employees with sick and vacation time, here are some steps that you should follow to ensure all is fair:

Be consistent. If you start giving one employee more leeway than the others you are bound to hear cries of unfair treatment, not to mention a dip in employee spirits.

Make advanced scheduling a requirement. Of course there are always going to be emergencies, but requiring advanced scheduling will help make sure your store is always appropriately staffed. It will also help cut back on sick day misconduct and remind employees that sick days are not free-for-alls.

Use a vacation accrual system versus flat out vacation days. The choice is ultimately yours here. If you want to provide a one week vacation, that is fine. However, another option for you is to setup an accrual policy, allowing employees to save up their days. For example, giving about an hour vacation time for every full working day will be about one to one and a half vacation days per month. It is also wise to set a limit on how many days can be accrued.

Contrary to popular belief, employers also do not have to legally provide pregnancy leave for employees. There are however, a few states that require employees give paid time off if a woman is physically unable to perform their work duties because of pregnancy and childbirth, although this is typically paid by the state. Check with your state's rules to see where you fall in regard to pregnancy leave.

What the federal law does require falls mostly under the Family and Medical Leave Act (FMLA). FMLA calls for employers who fall under specific guidelines to allow up to 12 unpaid weeks of leave per year for workers who need to take time off for pregnancy or a serious medical issue.

Employers having to comply with FMLA must meet these three terms:

1. They employ more than 50 individuals, all of which live within a 75 mile radius. They must all be on payroll to be included in the total.

2. The employee asking for leave has worked for your company for at least one year.

3. The employee has worked at least 1,250 hours during their year on the job.

Most flower businesses will never see numbers up to 50, therefore most will not have to obey this law. Nevertheless, most employers do let pregnant staffers use vacation or personal days for pregnancy related time off. As long as they provide the required notice, there is no reason not to.

As a rule, if you provide any sort of medical leave for one employee, it must be constituted for them all. For example, if you give one employee permission for medical leave due to a sprained wrist, you must also give a mother-to-be time off or you can face discrimination claims.

It should also be noted that under federal law you must provide military leave, as well as time off for voting and to serve on jury duty.

IRS

If you have employees, you, as the owner of the business and employer, must hold a certain amount of income, social security, and Medicare taxes for them, which is a certain percentage based on information from the employee's W-4. As the employer, you must also match the exact amount. You will also have to pay for unemployment taxes.

Make sure you keep up with these payments. The IRS will send notices and if you oblige them, you will be caught up. If you do not, you will get hit with huge dividends, among other consequences like fines and, in worst case scenarios, jail time.

It is imperative if you are looking to hire employees that you constantly keep a running tab of how much more you are bringing in with them in opposition to all the fees that come along with them. By all means, if your business is growing like wildflowers and you cannot possibly handle the workload on your own, hire someone to help. Just make sure it is worth your while.

Customers

Today, anyone can sue anyone for anything, from a hot coffee they dumped on themselves to tripping over their own two feet and breaking their leg. If it happens in your store, they may try to sue. Make sure your in-store policies speak loud and clear and are hanging somewhere for all to see. Cover your tracks with the right insurance and legal paperwork (if applicable).

Be the kind of store owner you would want to be served by if you were on the other side of the counter. Often, if an accident happens and you are considerate, people will be less likely to sue. Conversely, watch what you say when you are being kind. If you make a statement like "I do not know why that rug is folded up in the middle of the floor. Someone must have kicked it over," a lawyer will use it against you in a court of law. Avoid unnecessary situations by keeping your shop clean and your paperwork updated so that if something does occur, there is no way for blame to be placed on you.

Decor

When decorating your shop, you can truly let your creative juices flow. Make sure you get necessities first and have fun with any leftover budget.

Flower Shop Needs

The following is a short checklist of what you will need for the shop to start. After the list, each item is discussed in more detail.

- ⊛ Coolers
  - ❀ Reach-in cooler
  - ❀ Walk-in cooler
- ⊛ Workspace
  - ❀ Sinks
  - ❀ Arranging tables

- ❀ Storage

- ❀ Lighting

- ❀ Flooring

❀ Check Out Area

  - ❀ Cash register

  - ❀ Impulse items

  - ❀ Counter space

❀ Nice Touches

  - ❀ Furniture and shelving

  - ❀ Greeting card rack

  - ❀ Theme

Coolers

Above any other equipment, two types of coolers, the walk-in and the reach-in, are a must for any flower shop.

Walk-in Cooler

You can find a price and size of walk-in cooler to suit your shop and budget. The location of your store will determine what will work. There are so many options, so even if your space is small, you will be able to find something that works for you. Find companies that specialize in walk-in coolers and have them install it. The cooler is an asset that should last the longevity of your floral career. Do not skimp; this is one of the most important investments you will make for your shop. The last thing you need is for flowers to wilt or perish before they even make it to the arranging table. Furthermore, do not fret if you do not plan on being in your retail space forever. Many new models are easy to move or even expand if you need extra space. Be sure to have it professionally cleaned at least once a year. You do not want any funny smells to linger on bouquets once they enter clients' hands.

As previously mentioned, the size of your store will determine how large your cooler will be. Try to get one as big as possible so you can accommodate any future growth. They come in such a large variety that you should not have any problems finding the perfect one for your store. You must consider that a new one will cost a few thousand dollars. If you do not want to buy one, there are other alternatives, like renting. There are also manufacturers who carry used models for a lower price, which might have been leftover from a store closing. You will also want to find a technician who can service your walk-in to ensure it is at peak performance for your perishables at all times.

Reach-In Cooler

The reach-in cooler is as important as the walk-in cooler. This cooler will sit in the store where customers mingle, so you might want to invest in one with a glass door and a nice appearance. The reach-in will also display your arrangements to show off your expertise to customers.

Make sure the cooler is stocked and attractive, since it is an eye-catching element in your store. They come in a large variety of finishes, such as stainless steel, black, or different wood grains. Choose one that suits your decor. Purchase appealing containers and change up the displays daily with fresh flowers. Most of them come with adjustable shelving, so switch up the physical display as much as possible to keep it looking new and fresh to regular customers.

Think ahead and use the reach-in to your advantage. If it is holiday time, remember that many people forget to order an arrangement ahead of time. They will often try to scramble to get something for their host, event, or home, so have holiday arrangements ready during these times. If you are a niche florist, use the reach-in to display your most beautiful arrangements until they are moved to their destination. You can also use the reach-in for easy access for regulars who come in to pick up a weekly arrangement. When they arrive at the store and see their display waiting for all eyes to see, their loyalty will run even more deeply since they know you thought of them.

Work Space

Having the right work space, setup in the right manner, saves time for any florist. In addition to the coolers, the work space should include sinks, the arranging table, storage, and shelving.

Sinks

For a florist, a wimpy sink will not cut it. Install a sizeable utility sink in your work area. Get the biggest you can fit in your work space — the longer and deeper the better. A double sink with two different depths is your best bet, but if you do not have the space, having one large, deep sink will work just as well.

The rest of the area surrounding the sink should be a flat working space. Flat space is a valuable asset because this is where you will cut most of your flowers for arrangements. You will also be washing supplies and will need space to lay them out to dry. A dishwasher in your sink area is also a handy tool to have around. Keep your trash can close by so it is easy to sweep excess materials into it. If you can afford it, installing a grinder in your sink is an extremely helpful asset. It makes cleaning up extra foliage materials easier, but a grinder is not imperative. If you have a limited budget, make sure the basics are all there, and if you have some money or room to spare, a dishwasher and grinder are nice, useful touches.

Arranging Table

Although you have a sink area with plenty of flat space, you are going to want an area separate from the sink called the arranging table. You will often lay down bouquets that are pre-wrapped in paper instead of in a vase, making a dry arranging area essential. Having this raised area beside your sink area allows easier access to both. If flat surfaces are limited, keep what you have available for your sink area and invest in a long island for arranging. This island can also provide an extra storage area in smaller spaces.

Wrapping can also be done in the check out area, but it is advised to keep all arranging in the back area. When wrapping in front of customers, you run the risk of getting water on other paper materials like gift cards, a check being written out, a customer's belongings, or on the customers themselves. It also seems more professional if you appear from the back room with everything already taken care of, rather than having to finish up the wrapping job in front of your customer.

Storage

Although your coolers will do most of the storing, you should make sure you have optional storage available for other supplies. A roomy closet, armoire, or even some shelving in the work room will do nicely. If you find that you are too stocked with supplies, especially ones that are only used on rare occasions, like Christmas decorations, a cheap offsite storage unit can be incredibly useful. You can move unwanted clutter and seldom used items to the unit, although you will want to make sure it is close enough to the shop that if the occasion arises, you are not trekking miles to find your supplies.

Lighting

Although having some permanent lighting fixtures is ideal, make sure you also have plenty of movable light. Even if you have track lighting installed, being able to move the heads around to spotlight different areas of the shop is ideal. Adding table and floor lamps to your decor is a good way to provide atmosphere. They are also easy to move, so if you setup a display in a seemingly darker area of the shop, you will always have the option of moving a lamp over to improve the light in that area. Make sure there is adequate lighting in general to ensure that neither you nor your customers ever have to strain.

Flooring

Most retail stores will have a hard surface of some type rather than carpet. Adding throw rugs will add some texture and interesting focus to your store. Make sure all added rugs are rubber backed to reduce the risk of tripping hazards.

Practical Pointer

Look out for your customers and you will cover your own back as well. If you add rugs, never stack them or cause a tripping hazard. Always be on the lookout for curled edges on throw rugs that need to be smoothed down or replaced. Move materials that can cause a potential hazard for a customer. Take precautionary measures to prevent a customer from becoming injured or trying to sue.

Checkout Area

A plainly marked checkout area is a necessity for your shop. Customers should know where the checkout counter is because it should always be clearly marked and used only for checkout purposes. Having a few small items that customers might buy on a whim is alright. On the other hand, it might be better to have a separate shelf or section close by the counter for these items. This will keep the area clutter free. You do not want your customers to feel uncomfortably cramped, have no room to put down their personal belongings, or be nervous that they may knock over displays while they are checking out.

A cash register is also a must-have checkout area item. A cash register can be bought for a fairly inexpensive price.

Basic function registers can be found at office supply stores for about $100. If you want to align your register with inventory tracking devices and enable it to work with credit card sales, you will need a more complex option with a computerized system and the right software. Having all of that might be more of a hassle than it is worth. As a result, starting with a simple register might be the way to go.

You will also want to consider the height of your checkout counter. Make sure it is not so tall that small customers have to stretch to hand you money, but not so low that customers have to bend over to pick up their purchases. Depending on the style of your store, a nice table can do the trick, especially if you do not have the funds to get a proper counter installed. An antique farm table or a more modern look should be all you need to get your checkout counter up and running.

Nice Touch

Furniture and Shelving

Furniture is an opportunity to let your creativity shine. You can repaint an old dresser you no longer use or pick one up cheaply at an antique shop and refurbish it. Not only can you display items on top of the dresser, you can also use the drawers for storage or pull some of them out to stack items or create a unique display. You do not have to have fresh arrangements on the furniture. You can use them to further develop the theme of your store. For example, if you are going for a country theme, placing some dried flowers, an old mirror, and an antique watering can on top of the display will help further create ambience through your store. There is no limit to how you can use furniture in your shop.

Furniture can also be used as seating. A smart use of furniture would be to form a little niche where you can go with customers to talk in a more private setting, especially if you are wedding florist who will have frequent meetings with clients. It seems a bit more formal than just standing or milling around the store while talking.

Greeting Card Rack

Greeting cards are the perfect accessory to your shop. They often go hand-in-hand with flower arrangements, since much of your business will be customers purchasing flowers for others. Do not have only preprinted cards, but have just as many blank options. You might often find yourself stuck with many leftover holiday cards that go unused for many months of the year. By having blank cards, you will not get stuck in that situation as often.

There are several options for greeting card racks. They come in a variety of finishes such as wood, plastic, or metal. You can even opt for a small one in your checkout area, if you have room. Typical floor spinner racks hold plenty of cards and take up only a small amount of space. If you go for a wall rack, choose one that is decorative, because it will become a part of your shop's atmosphere and decor.

Rotate the rack often so it always appears fresh. Keep cards out of direct sunlight to prevent fading and dust often. The last thing you want is to be have faded, dusty, dirty cards that no customers will want to purchase.

Practical Pointer

Always ask customers whether they want to purchase a greeting card with their bouquet. Gently nudge them in the direction of your greeting cards just to "take a look" and see if they can find a card that is perfectly suited for their bouquet or arrangement's function.

Theme

A store theme is imperative. It helps customers get an idea of what your store is about. For example, if you go with a country theme, you can incorporate aspects of country life throughout your store. Choose a logo, like a watering can, and include it in decor, on signage, and in other marketing materials. Customers will soon link the watering can symbol to your store, which is exactly what you want. A common mistake is mixing several different themes because that confuses customers on what the store is about. If you boast a country theme in marketing materials but you have an upper crust window display featuring sharp red, white, and black colors and roses, a customer looking for a country themed bouquet might turn around upon seeing your display, figuring you are pricey or are not a country type of shop.

Choose a theme that coincides nicely with your personality, fits well within your locale, and is relatable to your target customer base. Colors also have an extremely strong impact. If you want customers to keep it moving, then bold, startling colors will do the trick. Sometimes, though, these colors often evoke other, unwanted moods. For example, although yellow seems bright and cheery for the most part, it stirs up a sense of anxiety and is even quite startling to some people. Good neutral choices are tans, beiges, whites, and off whites. A relaxing color palette will often work well, with tranquil colors like blues and greens. It is your choice, so make your colors and your decor work for you, and your store will be attractive inside and out to customers.

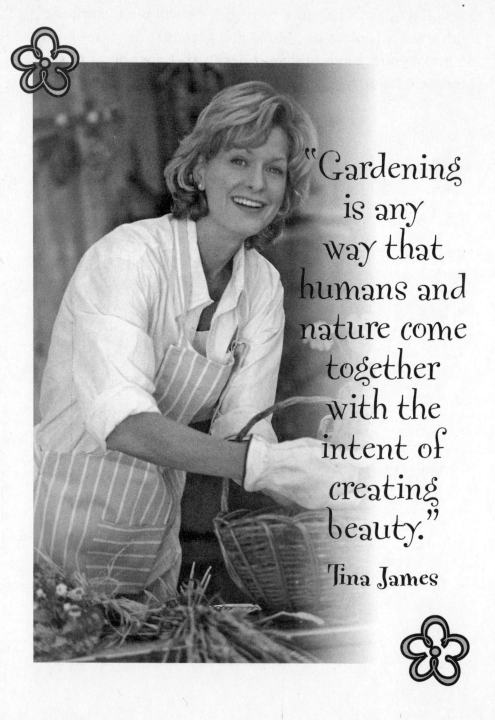

"Gardening is any way that humans and nature come together with the intent of creating beauty."

Tina James

The Product

Being a florist entails not only having a business savvy mind, but also a creative one. You must know your product inside and out. Knowing the most common flower types and having in-depth knowledge on many species is a huge plus. You never know what kind of questions customers will ask. Since most flowers are perishable, knowing how to care for them the right way is also important to any florist. Conversely, having the option of potted plants, foliage, and dried arrangements helps to expand your business to other customers who might not necessarily want flowers that will perish within a few days.

Common Products

Many customers are not up to speed on specifics like flower care, lifespan, care requirements, or what flowers work well with others. They will leave all of that up to you and will just expect a pretty finished product. Therefore, making smart choices, picking flowers with a lengthy cut life, and arranging flowers that coexist in an arrangement nicely is exceptionally important. If you are choosing dried flowers, they are arrangements that have no lifespan, but are awfully brittle and can fall apart easily; you will have to handle these with complete care. Here is a limited list of some of the most popular fresh flowers, foliage, and dried flowers and basic information about them.

Fresh Cuts

Roses: Roses are the number one selling flower in the country, and it is a not hard to see why. They are one of the most beautiful flower species and come in a large variety of colors. You might even say red roses — hearts and kisses aside — are the number one symbol of love. Yet, their vase life is extremely short — a week or even less. It is important to tell customers they must cut their roses before placing them in water. When choosing roses, pick ones that are not fully bloomed to further the lifespan of the arrangement.

Carnations: Carnations are a versatile flower. They come in a variety of colors, but can also be dyed easily to almost any color. They also have an exceedingly long vase life — up to two weeks — and are hardy and resistant.

Liatris: Liatris is an exceptionally basic flower which is often used as filler or to add some breadth to an arrangement. They have a long vase life and can last several weeks.

Lilies: Lilies are another customer favorite. They come in a stunning variety and many hues. They are also hardy and can last a few weeks if proper care is used, including trimming their stems every three days.

Freesia: Freesia is an incredibly fragrant flower for those who want a strongly scented bouquet, but they have an extremely minimal vase life of less than one week. They come in a large variety of bright colors.

Fillers: Filler is a general term for several different plant and flower species often used to fill empty spots in a bouquet or arrangement. This category includes several types of ferns and baby's breath, which is very popular.

Tropical: Tropical refers to foliage that naturally lives in a temperate climate. This includes a variety of gorgeous flowers including bird of paradise and plumeria. These flowers should not be kept in a temperature much lower than 55 degrees or they will perish.

Dutch: Dutch flowers are most commonly found during the spring. This group includes popular cuts such as tulips, daffodils, narcissuses, and irises.

Exotics: The exotic category holds some of the most striking flowers on earth. The most popular is the orchid. They are easier to care for than most think — with a little bit of patience and know-how. Many orchids are collector's items, so having a niche for exotics can be a lucrative business move. Vase life varies if these are cut.

Hydrangeas: Since they are bushy, hydrangeas work well when grouping. They come in a wide variety of colors and work well cut or dried.

Cornflowers: Cornflowers evoke a unique sense of "country," so they work exceedingly well in casual displays or in massed arrangements to provide a shot of color and depth. They also work well for boutonnieres and bouquets because of their bold color and compact, rounded shape.

Delphiniums: Delphiniums are exceptionally long and add great movement and height to arrangements, especially large-scale ones.

Calla Lilies: Calla lilies are a classic flower. They work wonders in formal displays, but with their thick stems and elegant shape, two or three callas grouped can add a nice touch to modern displays, too. You do not need many of these to make a strong impact.

Dahlias: Dahlias have an exceptionally solid shape and come in bold colors, so they often take over arrangements. If you do not want dahlias to be your focal point, do not put them in your display. They are statement makers.

Astilbe: With its wispy shape, astilbe is the perfect counterpart for bold flowers. They help maintain balance in arrangements and range in color from white to dark red.

Pinks: Pinks have an incredibly traditional look and are smaller than their carnation cousin. They add fragrance to an arrangement and are also extremely well-suited for boutonnieres.

Foliage

Hosta: Hosta is ideal for the base of any arrangement. Their smooth surface and strong shape make for attractive filler in arrangements.

Rosemary: Rosemary adds a nice silvery tone to foliage displays or flower arrangements. Longer-stemmed versions topple over beautifully while short-stemmed ones are good fillers. Rosemary adds a fragrant touch and can also be used for cooking purposes, since it is an herb.

English Ivy: English ivy is common in outdoor foliage and gardens. It is also popular in arrangements. It softens displays by evoking a sense of flow.

Eucalyptus: The eucalyptus has a clean, simple line, making it the perfect foil for more distinct flowers and foliage. It is a multitasker, but is a fantastic filler.

Bupleurum: Bupleurum is often used as a filler. It also adds contrast with its lime green coloring. It has a country, soothing appeal, great for casual displays.

Bear Grass: Bear grass is great for a minimal and contemporary arrangement. It has a classic shape and should be used sparingly. Bear grass can add great flow to an arrangement, especially when used in contrast to strong flowers, like lilies.

Butcher's Broom: Butcher's broom, also known as ruscus, can last up to four weeks when cut. There are several varieties, all of which lend a strong, curvaceous quality to displays.

Copper Beach: Copper beach is a debated flower. It offers a great alternative to traditional green foliage with its copper coloring, but its leaves wilt quickly. It should only be used when it is in peak season.

Dried Flowers

Lavender: Lavender emits a soothing smell and provides a rich color to dried displays. Its fragrant scent can last for months after it is dried out.

Roses: Roses keep their faint scent after they are cut. They are available in such a large variety that it is easy to find one to suit your arrangement. For the best dried roses, cut the stems before the blooms have fully opened.

Globe Artichokes: Globe artichokes are incredibly striking and bold in arrangements and often provide a strong focal point. They can stand their ground in large displays, whether casual or formal.

Corncobs: Corncobs add a rustic touch to modern or country displays. When dried, they provide a radiant golden color to arrangements and add a good bit of texture with seeds, steams, and leaves. Secure chicken wire horizontally and support the cob upright in the leaves to dry.

Sunflowers: A much loved flower, sunflowers work well in dried displays. Their large size allows them to stand out, but their soft colors are a cheery attention-getter in any display. They provide a lot of interest to any type of display and are great as one or in mass.

Amaranthus: Amaranthus become straight when dried to provide an architectural look to displays. They come in lime green or rusty red, and their fuzzy texture adds warmth and softness to arrangements.

Poppy Pods: Poppy pods help add structure to arrangements with a smooth, oval shape and neutral colors. They also take well to spray painting in order to add some more color to dried displays.

Strawflowers: Strawflowers come in a striking range of vibrant colors. The wide, circular heads look brilliant when arranged in masses. They do, however, have weak stems and need to be incredibly securely wired, and sometimes even rewired.

Bacteria

If flowers had an arch enemy, it would be bacteria. If a strain of bacteria gets into your store, it can devastate your stock; it causes flowers to prematurely wilt. You can stop the problem with a few easy steps. Invest in the small packets that frequently come with flower bouquets. These packages are filled with preservatives that keep bacteria at bay so that cut flowers last longer. Keeping all of your containers, tools, and your workspace disinfected is also a good preventive measure. Some plants need additional spray-on preservatives.

Watering and Feeding

Watering and feeding are known as hydration and nutrients in the floral world. Making sure all of your plants are properly watered and fed is an important process. Sending them out into the world malnourished will lead to premature wilting.

Before the flowers get to your customers, they will need to be prepped. Some of your flower supplies will come in water and some will come without. Those without will need to be hydrated with solutions like Quick Dip. You will need to remove them from their boxes, cut the stems, remove certain petals (those that are dying, in some cases the guard petals or those that fall below the water line), re-hydrate flowers that are being prepared for dry shipping, and get flowers ready to go into the coolers. This prep work is also known as processing. Customers should also be informed that re-cutting flowers before they enter a vase at home and then a final time, two or three days after purchase, will add a few days to their vase life.

In Short: Buy preservative packets in bulk for your use and for customer use. Offer a packet with every bouquet or arrangement that leaves your shop. It will maintain the lifespan of your arrangements, along with the lifespan of your business.

Flowers need the right nutrients to survive. The pH level on cut flowers differs from that of uncut. Cut flowers should be at a pH level of three or four. This is another place where those little preservative packets come in handy. Not only do they help control bacteria, they also contain nutrients like sugar that enhance the flowers' lifespan.

Non-flower Supplies

Having a variety of non-flower supplies can add to your profit, especially during months when sales are often slow. Like the decor and window treatments, this is a part of your business where you can let your creativity shine by using nontraditional items as a signature touch. Of course, you will also want to have basic supplies such as:

⊛ Boxes

⊛ Bulk and packets of preservatives

⊛ Cleaning products

⊛ Containers for the coolers

⊛ Foam

⊛ Gift tags

⊛ Glue

⊛ Glue guns

⊛ Moss

⊛ Other containers for arrangements

⊛ Outer wrap

⊛ Plastic wrap

⊛ Ribbon

⊛ Scissors

⊛ Shears

⊛ Spray

⊛   Vases

⊛   Wire

⊛   Wreath forms

Arranging

The art of arranging is the place where your skill set shines as a florist and should be your source of pride. Although there are some general rules to follow, you should use these as a loose guideline. It is more important to let your creativity show through to differentiate yourself from the rest of the floral pack.

Flower Arranging Basics

There are several different styles of arranging and types of foliage and flowers to choose from. Before you begin arranging, you have to think of the result and the setting that the bouquet is going to be placed in. Is it formal, modern, or casual? Making these basic decisions and knowing where your flowers are headed will set the foundation for each arrangement. Examples and descriptions of some such arranging styles follow.

- ❀ **Potted Displays:** Potted displays look best when they are kept simple. Placing a single plant in a container of your choice may seem minimalist, but it can make a remarkable impact and will adapt easily in many settings.

Many florists do an arrangement first and choose the container second. Try to do it the other way around. Pick a container that coincides with whatever the setting the arrangement is going to land in — casual, modern, or formal. Having a container to go around and choosing flowers that will further enhance the vase will make for a well-rounded, natural-looking display.

- ❀ **Classic Formal Display:** Many classic things with formal flare, like a tuxedo, often have great detail and strong lines, but the products involved are often used sparingly. The same principal can be applied to floral arrangements. Using a limited amount of flowers — one or two species max — can create an incredibly strong yet elegant arrangement.

- ❀ **Country Style Display:** Country arrangements are known for their informality. Think of a meadow full of wildflowers out in the country. They are often random, but work well together. Incorporate the image into your arrangements. Stick with a color palette that works well together. Select a variety of flowers and foliage at random to provide a natural, understated element to the arrangement.

- ❀ **Modern Grouped Display:** Many customers like things that have a modern appeal. Use two or three of the same small, unique containers and add one type of flower that truly pops to each; this looks stylish and pulled together. The containers are just as important as the flowers to most customers looking for something contemporary.

⊛ **Large, Informal Dried Arrangement:** As with the country style display, a large, informal dried arrangement should also appear as unaffected as possible, as though the flowers were plucked from their natural environment and placed in the arrangement. Dried flowers run the risk of appearing stiff and lackluster. Turn the risk on its head by adding different texture and colors. Keep a true look by grouping flowers together, which also helps to intensify specific colors.

This list is not comprehensive, but gives an idea of what arrangements are all about and the large variety of them that should be available to your customers.

Color

One of the most important aspects of your arrangement is color. Beautiful color stories are one of the main reasons people love flowers so much in the first place. The color palette is similar to a first impression and is what customers will note immediately with an arrangement.

Experiment with different hues. Play mix and match. Even contrasting colors can produce an unexpectedly bold and vibrant arrangement. Get to know each color on a first name basis. For example, bold red gives a rich, luxurious feel while yellow has an extremely vibrant, cheery quality. You should also have a color wheel handy to choose primary, monochromatic, and complementary colors with ease.

⚘ **Primary Colors:** The primaries are blue, yellow, and red. Placing these colors together makes for an exceptionally striking arrangement and using softer versions will still produce a viable effect, but in a more subtle manner.

⚘ **Monochromatic Colors:** Monochromatic colors are all the same color, but in a variety of tones. Using a range of the same color — from the especially strong to the especially subtle hue — gives great depth to an arrangement.

⚘ **Complementary:** Complementary colors do just that, they compliment one of the three primary colors. Complementary colors do not use the primary that they complement in their makeup. For example, purple is mixed with a combination of the primaries blue and red, so it is a considered a complementary to yellow.

Many colleges, especially art colleges, offer color classes. It would not hurt to take one to further your knowledge on color since it is a main ingredient for arrangements.

Materials

When you are arranging flowers, you should know that there is incredibly basic equipment that is essential to long-lasting arrangements. These include:

⚘ **Butcher's Hooks:** Attaching these hooks to the back of arrangements allows them to be suspended from mantelpieces, tables, or other alternative surfaces.

- **Cement Mix:** Mixing cement mix with water allows materials to stay securely in place in pots. Line the pot with plastic before using the mix.

- **Chicken Wire:** Chicken wire is extremely useful because of its flexible yet strong nature. It is particularly helpful as a binder in providing extra support to loose displays or when making garland bases.

- **Clear Adhesive Tape:** This all-purpose tape is ideal for making support grids on bowls and vases. You can then stick flowers or foliage in the grid's gaps.

- **Cutting Tools:** Scissors are practical in cutting flowers and wire. A knife can be helpful in stem preparation by eliminating bumps and superfluous materials.

- **Dry Foam:** Dry foam is helpful in dried displays and should always be used dry. It comes in many shapes, like blocks or cones, and can be cut if need be.

- **Fine Florist's Tape:** This tape is thin and rubber based. It seals extremely well under heat or pressure, making it ideal for binding or hiding wire.

- **Florist Wire:** Florist wire is thin but strong. It gives support to delicate and/or long arrangements in particular. It comes in many lengths and gauges.

The finest comes in 30 gauge, while the thickest used is usually a 90 gauge. It also comes in different metals, making it easier to hide.

⚜ **Florist's Foam:** Oasis, as it is called in the industry, is the green florist foam nearly everyone has seen before in fresh flower arrangements. Float the foam in water with nutrients and add it to fresh cut flowers only.

⚜ **Florist's Tape:** This tape is exceedingly strong and waterproof. It sticks to nonporous and shiny surfaces, making it ideal for use on metal plates or florist's foam.

⚜ **Foam Ring:** This is less sturdy than the copper wreath frame, but is helpful in hydrating fresh flower displays. It can also be used in dried displays.

⚜ **Glue:** Although you do not want to use glue all the time, it is helpful when attaching awkward materials, such as shells, to arrangements or containers.

⚜ **Plastic Bowls:** Bowls are useful protection in case of a container leak. They are placed beneath the container and can also be used as a decorative element.

⚜ **Plastic:** Many times, surfaces need better protection from water and soil. This is where plastic comes in. It is useful in lining garlands, wreaths, and the inside of pots.

- **Saucer:** Saucers can be attached to rings while wet in fresh cut floral arrangements. The saucer can also be placed in larger containers to provide water.

- **String:** String works well in binding situations, and it can also be used as a decorative element in arrangements.

- **Wreath Frame:** These copper wire frames are used for attaching flowers and foliage when making a wreath.

- **Wreath Wrap:** Wreath wrap is merely a thin strip of plastic that is ideal for wreaths and garlands.

It is also good to have these tools for emergency purposes:

- Desk stapler

- Hammer

- Pliers

- Screwdriver

- Spray bottles

- Staple gun

Skills

There are several skills that will help flower arranging become easier if you can get a firm grasp them.

Preparing and Treating

When you are arranging for clients, you simply cannot just plop flowers in a vase. The proper preparations and treatments must be done to make sure your arrangement lasts long and maintains a fresh look.

Prepping Stems

The first order of business when getting flowers ready for arranging is to properly prep the stems. First, break off all the leaves that will sit below the waterline; this helps keep the water fresh and also makes the overall appearance cleaner. Next, scrape down the stems with a small knife to smooth them out, remove old tissue, and to rid them of thorns. Finally, cut the bottom of each stem on a diagonal to provide a bigger surface space for maximum water absorption. This last step also creates a small point that makes it easier to put stems into florist foams and vases.

 **Practical Pointer**   By cleaning and cutting your stems properly, you are promoting better water uptake and making the flowers more aesthetically pleasing.

Plugging Hollow Stems

Many flowers, like the amaryllis, are hollow-stemmed, which can often lead to early wilting. To promote better water uptake, you will want to fill hollow-stemmed flowers with water and plug them at the bottom; doing so is easy. Hold the stems upside down and fill them with as much water as they can take. Put a swab of cotton into the hollow to hold in the water. This also allows the flower to soak up water once it is in the arrangement.

Straightening Stems

In nature, flower stems do not always come perfect and straight. More often than not, they will need to be hand straightened to maintain a streamlined look. Once the stems are properly prepared, wrap them in a brown paper bag or similar material. Tie the bundle with tape or string. Next, put the stems in fresh water for several hours, although overnight is best. Within that time, they will soak up enough water to fully straighten.

Conditioning

Flowers need food, too. This will help hold off on the wilting period or if they have already begun to wilt, conditioning will revitalize them. Protect flowers by covering them with brown paper. Put the stems in warm water and saturate the water with a packet of plant food. The warm water is an important part of conditioning because it blocks air bubbles that might otherwise prevent the water and nutrients from reaching the flower heads. Let the flowers stay in the water for several hours. You can even do this step during the straightening period since the flowers will already be properly bundled.

Practical Pointer

According to the American Floral Endowment, flowers need a high concentration of carbohydrates to survive properly. "Pulsing" flowers often helps maintain longevity in cut flowers. Simply place them in a sugary mixture for a short period (24 hours or less) at a lower temperature.

Cleaning Petals

Several flower species have stamens that leak and stain profusely. To avoid staining the petals and your clothing, you will want to remove these parts, which is an easy process. Gently pull the stamen from its stalk with your finger and dispose of them immediately. These parts need to be removed before they reach maturity or staining will be unavoidable.

Preserving Plants

When preserving any plant material or flower, you begin the processes as quickly as possible to preserve maximum color and prevent decay. Many florists use any of the three following processes to preserve their plants.

Air Drying

Air drying is the easiest way to preserve plants; though you must note that it is not for every plant and flower. To start, pick flowers several days before they reach their prime. Make sure the weather is dry, as the process will not work as well with wet or damp flowers. Remove the lower portion of the leaves and spiral the stems to make as much space between each flower head as possible, allowing maximum airflow. Bind the bundle with string and hang it in a temperate, well-ventilated, darkened room for approximately one week.

In Short: According to the Neil-Reid study, bacteria and yeast, among other microbes, thrive on most flowers. To cut the risk of disease due to these microbes, clean all storage units like buckets and tubs before placing new flowers in them. You can also add anti-microbe solutions to further reduce the risk. Sanitation is a major key.

Glycerin

Glycerin is a better option than air drying for some flowers, such as lilies that have woody stems and for many forms of foliage. The plants will remain supple but may undergo a hefty color makeover during the process. To start, mix a solution of 50 percent hot water and 50 percent glycerin in a vase. Place your bundle into the solution for at least a week and then remove and wash.

Silica Gel

Silica gel works well to draw excess moisture out of flowers, giving them a "fresh flower" look. Simply:

1. Pour a layer of gel into a container.

2. Put the flowers in it, and cover with a lid.

3. Once the lid is on, seal it with tape and leave it for a week or more.

All the necessary aids for plant preservation can be found at a local craft store and sometimes even a floral shop.

Spiraling

A profound knowledge on the spiraling technique will get you far as a florist for three reasons. First, it creates a bunch that is easier to hold; second, it gives support to the stems; and third, it simply looks better. There are two ways to spiral stems — through a bound bouquet or hand-held spiraled bouquet. Let us take a closer look.

Bound Bouquet: Start with your first stem. Hold it about halfway down from the head. Add a second stem and angle it diagonal. Do the same with the third and then bind them with a string. Continue the hold, angle, angle, bind pattern until you are about halfway finished. You can start adding two or three flowers at a time at this point and binding them once around each time you add more. Keep the "waist" as slender as possible. When you are finished, tie the string in a knot or bow. Make sure it is strong enough that all of your efforts do not come undone. Trim the bottom of all the stems flat so that the entire bouquet is able to stand freely. Cover the original string with a matching bind or bow.

Hand-held Spiraled Bouquet: You will start this type of spiraled bouquet in a similar manner as the bound, yet, when you start adding flowers, you will want to still angle diagonally, but always to the left of the previous stem. Continue to add and hold in place with your own fingers, making sure the distance from one head to the other is the same. When you are finished, trim all the stems evenly and put the bouquet in a vase.

Wiring

All the wires that florists use come in various gauges for a combination of reasons. Most heavy wires, like 71 or 90 gauges, are used as hairpin hooks and double leg mounts, and work to secure items to the base of the arrangement.

Medium wires, like 56 gauge, are often used to support delicate dried flowers. The finest wires work well in reinforcing fragile flowers and leaves, or creating flexible stems. Wires are not limited to these jobs alone so you can use them as creatively as you like. The following is a mixture of different wiring techniques.

⚜ **Hairpin Hooks:** To make a hairpin hook, simply bend a heavy gauge into a hook by holding it in the center and taking the two ends together so they are parallel to one another. When using the hairpin hook to secure an object to the arrangements base, push the hook down into the arrangement until it is firmly in the base.

⚜ **Double Leg Mounts:** Using a heavy gauge, hold the wire in a horizontal manner behind the stem. Make sure the stem hits the center and bend the ends up so they run parallel to the stem. Take the right section of the wire and bend it across the stem front and over the left section of wire. Twist it around the left wire two to three times and then run it parallel to the left wire, creating the double leg.

⚜ **Wiring Flower Heads:** Cut off the stem about a half inch beneath the flower head. Put a heavy wire into the head where the stem once stood. Next, drive a fine wire into one side of the base of the head through to the opposite side. With precision, pull the fine wire through the head so it is even on both sides. Bend the two ends down so they lie parallel with the heavy wire. Loop the right section of thin wire around the left hand section two to three times and then bring it parallel to the other wires. Trim off the ends of the finer strands.

- ❀ **Wiring a Single Leaf:** Gently thread a fine wire through the main vein in the back portion of the leaf, approximately one-third of the way from the top. Make sure that both sides are even and pull both stands downward. Pass the left hand wire over the stalk and twist it two to three times around the right section and stalk.

- ❀ **Wiring a Trio of Leaves:** Thread the right hand and middle leaves on the stem separately and then trim off the excess wire. Wind the left hand leaf in the same manner and then twist the left hand section of wire around the steam and the other wire legs.

In Short: According the Neil-Reid study, many of the most common flower diseases can only infect a flower through an injury point. Be extra careful when it comes to breakage.

Wiring Specific Flowers and Foliage

Some flowers and foliage need a bit more coaxing to be wired correctly. Some of the most common differing flowers and foliage and how to wire them correctly follow.

- ❀ **Delphinium:** Delphiniums often need extra assistance. Each flower can be supported with a fine gauge wire by pushing the wire through the stalk below the flower head and twisting it into a double leg mount.

⊛ **Nerine:** To wire a nerine, cut the stem a half inch below the head of the flower. Push a fine wire through the base of the head and twist it around the short stem until it forms a double leg mount.

⊛ **Dried Acheillea and other Similar Dried Flowers:** To secure dried acheillea into dry foam, remove the sprigs from the main stem and bind two or three sprigs together with a medium gauge wire. Bend it into a double leg mount.

⊛ **Freesia:** Begin by cutting the stem a half inch below the flower head. Starting at the base of the stem, wrap the wire around the flower and wind it between each bud. Wind the wire back down around the buds. When you reach the original starting point, push the wire into a double leg mount. Fine floral wire is too short for most freesia wiring, so you will need a reel of wire to do this properly.

⊛ **Gladiolus:** Remove excess buds except for the main flower head. Push a heavy gauge wire through the head and thread a fine wire through the bud. Twist the finer of the two into a double leg mount.

⊛ **Daisy Head:** Cut the stem to about three-quarters of an inch below the flower head. Push a heavy gauged wire into the steam and up through the head. Thread a fine wire through the bud and twist the fine wire into a double leg mount.

⊛ **Lily of the Valley:** More often than not, the leaves of Lily of the valley need extra support. To add this, push a heavy gauge wire through the stem of an individual leaf. Thread fine wire through the main vein on the backside of the leaf and end about one-third of the way from the top. Even out both sides and bend the ends downward. Thread them both through the vein about a one-third of the way from the bottom of the leaf in such a way that the wires cross. Bring the ends down and twist them into a double leg mount.

- ✿ **Parrot Tulip:** Begin by pushing a heavy wire through the stem of the tulip. Make sure your wire has some length or you may run out. Cover another long wire with fine florist's tape and leave about three-quarters of an inch uncovered. Push the uncovered segment into the stem below and into the flower head. Wind the tape-covered wire around the stem and twist it into a double leg mount.

Binding Wired Stems

By binding wired flowers and leaves with fine green florist's tape, you are making the flowers much easier to work with while concealing unsightly wires. The tape is extremely flexible and seals with pressure and a bit of heat. It can also be split down the middle when working with intricate materials, like a wedding bouquet, to make it even finer.

- ✿ **Binding Single Stems:** Begin by holding the tape down just below the leaf. Turn the stem steadily so the tape winds down over the wires. Make sure it is overlapping itself each turn. Break off the tape firmly with your fingers when you reach the bottom of the wires. The heat and pressure of your fingers alone will be enough to seal the tape at the end of the wires.

⊛ **Combining Bound Stems:** Hold an already bound leaf stem against an already bound flower stem. Press the end of the fine florist's tape just below the flower head and twist the flower and leaf so the tape begins to bind the two together. Continue with another leaf. Place the second leaf against the bound flower stem and rotate the trio until the tape covers the entire length of all the steams. Twist off the tape at the bottom to seal.

⊛ **Making a Unit:** Units are traditionally made up of several independently wired items that are attached along a main stem and bound by floral tape in a manner similar to the combining bound stems segment. They are commonly used for large arrangements. Begin by wiring and binding the longest stem in the group. This item will set the tone and length of the entire arrangement. Hold your next pre-bound item to it at the point where they are both bound and tape them together with a few rotations of fine florist's tape. Make certain they maintain a parallel appearance. When adding more elements, work toward yourself. Bind on the next piece directly below the binding point of the item before it, to the right of the stem. Alternate left and right as you add more components and continue binding immediately beneath the last item. Continue keeping the stems parallel to maintain a thinner, more aesthetically pleasing look. When you are finished adding on or the group looks full, bind all the stems together with tape to form a handle. Break off the tape at the end and seal it. This one group can be attached to others to form a larger entity or can be left alone to work as a bouquet.

※ **Binding a Bouquet with Ribbon:** Bind the ribbon around the top of the stems, making sure to leave an ample tail. Coil it down so it overlaps itself. At the bottom of the stems, tuck the ribbon up under the end of the stems and press it into the side of the group. Wind the ribbon back up around the stems, making sure to secure the freshly done tuck at the bottom. Spiral and overlap while winding up the stalk. Once you have reached the tail at the top, tie the ends in a knot and cut the ends to the require length on a slant.

Making Bows

Bows can be used in a variety of ways by florists. They can liven up a display or add a punch of needed color to a muted palette. They can also add movement to dried arrangements and can cover up wires, tape, or binding. There are two common bows that are used in flower arranging — single and double. Let us take a look at how to do each.

※ **Single Bow:** Pinch the fabric in the center with your left hand while taking the right tail back through the center to form a loop. Hold the newly formed center point with your right hand. Take an identical amount of fabric from the left tail and bring it to the middle to form the second loop. Hold the newly formed center point with your left hand. Hold a heavy gauge wire behind the center point. Curve the top down over the center and twist to form a double leg mount. Cut the tails to the appropriate length on a slant. Use the wires as needed.

⊛ **Double Bow:** Use twice the amount of ribbon you would when doing a single bow. Follow the same steps until the point where you are to grab the second loop with your left hand. Bring the right hand tail back to the center to form another loop and hold the center point with your right hand. Now bring some ribbon from the left hand and tail back around to the center to form yet another loop on the left side. Cross a short piece of fabric over the center point, then wind a heavy gauge wire around the tails to form a double leg mount. Trim the tails on the centerpiece of ribbon. Cut the tails of the bow on a slant. Use the double leg mount as a hook or as necessary.

Once you have gotten a handle on these basic skills, you can expand from here to create beautiful bouquets, intricate detailed works, and large arrangements.

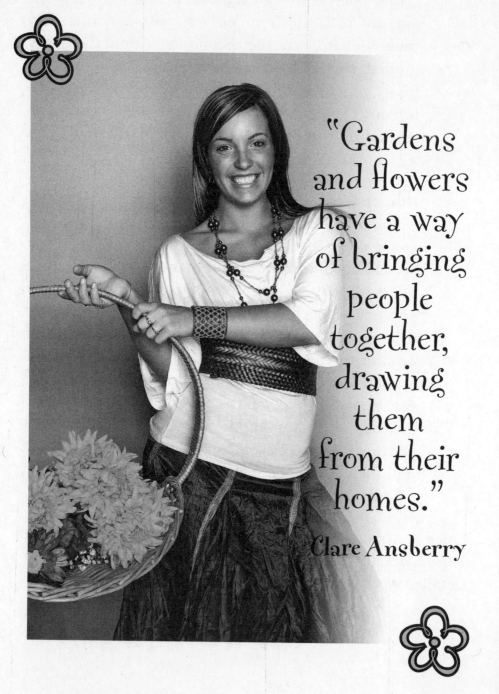

"Gardens and flowers have a way of bringing people together, drawing them from their homes."

Clare Ansberry

The Ins & Outs of Daily Business

Although every business is not the same, most florists follow a similar daily routine to ensure every aspect of commerce is well taken care of.

Rise and Shine

Once you have arrived at and opened the store, there are several things that should be done right away, or they are more often than not lost until the following day due to a heavy schedule or a lot of in and out of the store traffic.

Getting Ready

As soon as you arrive and step foot in the store, you should go to the front of the store and make sure it is customer ready. A fresh pair of eyes might catch a crumpled rug that is a trip hazard more easily. Furthermore, it is hard to find time during the day once you get going to make it to the other side of the counter to clean up the customer area of the store. Make sure arrangements are moved around in the coolers for a new look. Clean up any messes or spills. Empty trash cans. Wipe down windows. Do any clean up duties that you see fit to ensure you are not cleaning up the front when the first customer walks through your door.

Messages

Next, you will want to check all messages on your telephone and electronic mail. Write down every order detail on a notepad. Once you have gotten all of your messages down, number order them so you can get a prioritized list ready. For example, if a customer is coming in at 9 a.m. sharp to pick up a small bouquet while another is coming in two days from now for a funeral arrangement, you should do the small bouquet first.

Organize

Keeping yourself organized is a large key to having a successful day. Once your daily cleaning and message taking is out of the way, focus on organizing. Prioritize your to do list, remembering to add in the new messages you just took. Prepare your workspace. Make sure everything is in its proper place so you do not become frazzled or panicked because of a lost pair of scissors or a misplaced order.

You might also want to get used to multitasking as part of your organization skill set. It is important to be able to multitask so if you are in the back arranging and a customer walks through the front door, you can handle the customer and get back to business in a quick, efficient, and friendly manner, leaving the customer satisfied and yourself together. The worst thing that can happen is to become unnerved every day when something does not go according to schedule or an influx of customers comes through the door. If you plan on hiring employees, be sure to ask if they are efficient multitaskers so they can help take some of the weight off of your shoulders.

Orders

Orders make your business go round. Having a good handle on the large variety of order types that may be thrown your way throughout the day will increase your odds of being able to juggle the lot with ease.

Special Occasion

Florists must always have a good handle on what holidays or special occasions are approaching on the calendar. Preparations should be made well in advance for these particular days, even upward of one to two months. An easy way to see what was used the previous year is by calling vendors to see what was ordered during that time. You will also want to look at current records to see if your numbers or going up and what your funds are like. This should give you a good idea of what stock and supplies to order and exactly how much. Special occasions like Valentine's Day and Christmas always see an increase in sales numbers due to a flood of customers, so be prepared for the rush to make certain you create return clients, even if it is just once or twice a year.

Phone and E-mail Orders

When you walk into your shop in the morning, the second thing on your "to do" list after getting customer ready should be to check your phone and electronic mail messages. Check wire orders that might come over via Teleflora, FTD, or other wire ordering services; have a pad handy to jot down all orders. Be sure to include the customers' name, phone number, and exactly what they want. If you have any questions, do not hesitate to give them a call to ensure they get what they paid for. In addition, respond to any e-mailed questions from customers promptly. Integrate the new order list with other older orders that might have been placed several days before delivery.

Walk-Ins

During all of your morning preparation and arranging, keep your ears open for walk-ins. As the old saying goes "customers come first," so put down whatever it is that you are doing and attend to walk-in customers first. Walk-ins can certainly be an important part of your business and can also be the first step in achieving a new, loyal customer.

 **Statistic %** Nearly 67 percent of people who purchase flowers are simply purchasing for themselves, according to a study by the American Floral Endowment.

Deliveries

When speaking in terms of deliveries, there are two types, the kind coming in and the kind going out. The deliveries that are coming in are often supplies and fresh flowers to stock your store. The types that are going out are the ones being seen directly by the eyes of your clients. Whether you are hand delivering, have a hired delivery person, or go through a delivery service, it is important to always be on top of deliveries so they go out and are received on time, every time. Outgoing deliveries are certainly one of the points that will make or break your shop's good name.

Practical Pointer

A global positioning system, or GPS, is a good thing to have installed into your delivery vehicle. In the long run, this tool will save you time and, in due course, money. Make sure to read the handbook and get to know your GPS component so you can truly reap the benefits of it.

When you are arranging for a special occasion and preparing for delivery, it is always nice to throw in a personal touch to show how much you care, while keeping in mind that upward of a few hundred people may see your work if it is a large gathering or event. For example, if you are delivering for a funeral, be sure to send your condolences with a smaller, personal arrangement, specifically from your store, to the grieving. Although it is a sad situation and you feel sorrow for the anguished party, you are also running a business and must remember all the eyes that will see your arrangements that day.

A Day Filling Orders

Although there have been times when you might have been in other flower shops and the owner was out front, ready to greet you, this impression is simply not the case in any ordinary day at the flower shop. That florist probably spent 90 percent of their day behind the scenes, as will you.

If you are a one-person show, you should be ready to take on all the above, which includes phones, walk-ins, orders, deliveries, vendor drop-offs, and daily clean up, among many other things. When it comes to arranging and filling your day to maximum capacity, while taking on all of these tasks, it is helpful to have multitasking skills at hand. Whether you take a class to gain better focus or read a book on multitasking, using this skill is imperative to juggling day-to-day life as a florist.

When your budget allows, consider hiring an employee to unload some of the burden of daily life. They can work in many areas or solely in one, but whatever they do, be sure they are a great multitasker, too.

Pricing

When you are determining pricing for your orders, there are several factors to consider:

- Is the item perishable, a hard good, or a mixture of both?

- How do I markup the price from what I paid to what the customer pays?

- How do I incorporate charges to pay myself?

- What happens if my rent goes up or other costs need to be reflected in the order?

- How much should I charge if I am also setting up the arrangements for specific orders?

❀ Is there a delivery cost that should be incurred by customers?

Although these seem like swirling questions, here is an easier breakdown of answers so that you can set the right pricing for yourself and your customer base.

Pricing for Perishables and Hard Goods

Even though you are trying to make money, you have to always remember that your product is perishable. As a florist, you need to have a quick selling turnaround to ensure you make a profit. Otherwise, your goods will become damaged or die and you will be at a loss. Due to this, you have to price your perishables differently than you price your hard goods.

Markup Basics

How you determine what price tag to place on an item is based on markup. By **Dictionary.com**'s definition, markup is the amount added by a seller to the cost of a commodity (the flowers) to cover expenses (supplier costs) and profit (labor fees) to fix the retail price (price the customers will pay).

There are some basic rules that most florists follow when they are determining markup:

❀ **Fresh Flowers:** Since these are the most perishable goods in a flower shop, florists normally mark these up from 200 to 400 percent, depending on the type of flower and their availability. For example, a flower that costs $1 wholesale should be marked up to a retail price of $3 to $5.

- ❀ **Plants:** Plants are also perishable items, although they may be potted and have a lower risk of expiring. Regardless, they are normally marked up 200 to 300 percent. Therefore, a plant that costs $10 when you buy it wholesale should cost $30 to $40 retail.

- ❀ **Hardware:** Hardware includes items like pots, cards, or giftware. These are nonperishable and should be marked accordingly at 100 to 150 percent. An example would be a pot that cost $10 wholesale would be sold for approximately $20 to $25 retail.

- ❀ **Artificial Flowers:** Although these are not perishable, they are still usually marked up to about 200 percent of wholesale prices. An artificial rose that $1 wholesale should sell for about $3 retail.

❀ Sample Pricing List ❀	
Product	**Price**
Flowers	
Anthruriums	$3.50 / stem
Birds of Paradise	$7.25 / stem
Carnations	$1.50 / stem
Chrysanthemums	$1.75 / stem
Daffodils	$2.98 / every 3 stems
Freesias	$2.00 / stem
Gerber Daisies	$1.50 / stem
Gladiolus	$2.00 / stem
Irises	$2.98 / every 3 stems
Liatris	$1.50 / stem
Oriental Lilies	$7.00 / stem
Roses	$4.00 / stem $48 / dozen
Tiger Lilies	$2.00 / stem

❁ Sample Pricing List ❁	
Tulips	$2.98 / every 3 stems
Sunflowers	$4.00 / stem
Snapdragons	$2.50 / stem
Plants	

Cacti
  4" Pot
  8" Pot
	
	$5.50 to $10.50
	$20.50 to $40.50

Flowering	
Azaleas	$35.00
Begonias	$20.00
Chrysanthemums	$20.00
Gerber Daisies	$25.00
Hydrangeas	$40.00
Lilies	$30.00
Zygocactus	$30.00
* Note: All Flowering plants come in 6" pots only	
Green Tropical	
4" Pot	$3.50 to $4.50
6" Pot	$8.50 to $13.50
8" Pot	$15.50 to $30.50
10" Pot	$35.50 to $55.50
Hard Goods	
6" Wicker Basket	$3.00
10" Wicker Basket	$5.00
Florist Foam	$0.99 / brick
6" Glass Vase	$5.00
10" Glass Vase	$9.00
Specialty Vase	$12 to $25
Other	
Balloons	$1.00 / balloon

Stuffed Animals
  Small
  Medium
  Large
	
	$8.00
	$15.00
	$22.00

❀ Sample Pricing List ❀	
Candles	
Taper	$3.00 to $6.00
Pillar	$12.00 to $25.00
Cards	
Greeting	$3.00 to $5.00
Enclosure	Free with purchase

In Short: As a rule of thumb, retailers often mark items down a few pennies less than their calculations. For instance, if you have an item that you have marked up to $9, you will want to consider knocking off a few pennies and selling it for $8.99 or $8.95. Lessen the mark up but stick with the same ending throughout the store to unify items.

Incorporating Labor Fees

The simple markup is not the end of the road for retail pricing. You also have to pay yourself and consider some additional costs, like renting arches for a wedding that may crop up over time.

Labor fees often hang around 30 percent in North America, give or take a few percentage points. When determining labor fees based on 30 percent labor costs, you will first use the preceding prices and get the retail price. Multiply that retail price by 30 percent, or 0.3, and add the value onto the first retail price calculation.

Formula example:

If the total cost of all of your materials used and your first markup is $25, you will multiply that by 30 percent.

$25 Markup x 30 percent Labor Charge = $7.50 Labor Cost

Next, add the labor cost to the top of the original $25.

$25 Markup + $7.50 Labor Cost = $32.50 Retail Price

You have your retail price of $32.50, which covers material and labor costs.

For special occasion preparations, such as intricate wedding corsages or large funeral arrangements, most florists prepare a special labor price, since they are often more demanding projects. The average percentage is customarily 50 percent and retail pricing can be acquired through the same formula.

On the other side of the coin, if a smaller arrangement is required, like a simple one-flower, one-stem boutonniere for wedding groomsmen, charge a lesser fee of about 20 percent. Being flexible with customers will come back to you tenfold.

Rental Costs

You will come across niche clients that want decorated archways, pergolas, or other large structures, but do not want to purchase them for the occasion. In these instances, it is always good to have some of these items on-hand to rent out or to have a vendor that will rent them out to you for a reasonable price. You can then add the rental cost on top of the arrangement's retail price.

For example, if you own a small pergola that cost you $600 to buy, you can rent it to your clients at a percentage of that cost. A customary rental percentage is about 10 percent, making the rental cost $60 to your client.

Formula Example:

> $600 Purchase Price X 10 percent Rental Fee = $60 Cost to Client

You can either ask for a deposit upfront or add it on to the charge of the entire arrangement for the pergola.

If you do not have the means to store such items, have a vendor on-hand who has them readily available. You can do the work for the client to get the item rented. You can figure out the retail price of this easily by adding on the rental fee plus a 10 percent labor rental fee.

Formula Example:

You should first figure out what the labor fee is to the client if you do the work for them.

> $50 Rental Price from Vendor X 10 percent Labor Fee = $5 Labor Fee

Next, add the labor fee onto the rental price.

> $50 Rental Price from Vendor + $5 Labor Fee = $55

Do not over charge for minor details such as this, but rather look at it as a kind way to aid a client who may be in need of help. Their loyalty will be the ultimate payback.

Setup Fees

Sometimes as a florist, you will be asked to setup arrangements. Be sure to include incurred costs such as setup time, fuel costs, and the number of people required.

A good starting point is about $50 per hour, give or take. You can use this as a flat rate no matter what or you can use your best judgment and base the figure on the intricacy of the job. For example, if you are simply placing arrangements on the head and guest tables, you may want to charge less. If you are building or installing a large structure, you might want to charge more.

Also, make sure that you fill in your client if you are posting additional charges to the bill for any setup. This will avoid confusion in the long run if they know what each penny is being spent on.

Incoming

Throughout the day, you will have an influx of people and flowers running through your shop. From suppliers to wholesale florists to delivery trucks, "incoming" traffic will be a big part of any florist's day.

Suppliers

When you start your search for suppliers, think local.

Although some flowers will have to be imported, order as much inventory from locally grown wholesale markets and greenhouses as you can. By establishing a good relationship with a local vendor, the goodwill can come back to you tenfold if you are in need of a rush order or have run out of your inventory supply for the day.

With today's technology, you can also purchase stock online from vendors around the world. The plus to this is that you can offer flowers not normally found in your region; the obvious downfall being that the inventory can become costly. To make sure you are buying from a reliable source, make sure that any non-local vendor you buy from is affiliated with either an American or international floral association.

Statistic %

According to the American Floral Endowment, the floral industry comes in third in the agricultural industry, only trailing corn and soybeans.

However you choose to go about finding a vendor, most are easily accessible when it comes to orders with today's technology. You can usually find a place that will permit you to order online or over the phone, allowing you to choose the method you are most comfortable with.

For most florists, the first few stocks of inventory will be considered an out-of-pocket expense. Once you start to establish a working relationship with one or two vendors, they may offer you a small line of credit. From here, other vendors will take a look at these credit lines and will offer you additional funds, which in turn will allow you to grow your business. When it comes to vendor relations, being open, honest, and, most importantly, on time every time will allow for a fruitful relationship.

Growers

Let us start at the beginning of where your deliveries come from. Their first home is with a grower. Growers have massive quantities of flowers and plants they sell to floral wholesalers, market places, or directly to retail florists. Most often, flowers and plants are grown in greenhouses that sometimes stretches for acres on end or in giant fields. They are then harvested just before they are in bloom so they will carry on until they reach the end consumer.

If this is your niche, you will almost certainly have a constant flow of incoming trucks filled to the brim with your product. But before they make the journey, you will have to sort your harvest by color and variety, bundling them in large bunches, sometimes up to 25 stems at a time. You will have to choose which shipping method works best for each bundle; either the "wet," when flowers are shipped in huge water-filled containers, or "dry," when they are stored in giant truck- or plane-sized coolers.

You can sell directly to florists if you like but more often than not, most of your stock will be going to wholesalers or flower markets. Most growers only allow large quantities to be bought and have rigid minimums set so that time and money are not wasted. You will have to decide whether you want to sell to retail florists directly and, if so, what type of policies you will set for them since they are characteristically an extremely different type of customer than a wholesaler.

If you are a grower, make sure you sign on with as many wholesalers and markets as you can. Having a constant flow of incoming and outgoing trucks full of your flowers and greens is important in maintaining the flux of your business.

Wholesale Flower Deliveries

Most wholesale florists have a long, busy day that starts very early. Many operate near a flower market, where they go early (sometimes at 3 a.m.) to look at the stock and pick what they need that day for their retailers. The wholesalers will then load up their delivery van and head out for a day of deliveries to all of their retailers, who are most likely also in their locale. Other wholesalers have deliveries coming in directly from growers into their warehouse. Most often, deliveries come anywhere from every day to a few times a week, depending on the stock they have chosen to sell.

Wholesalers offer quite a variety and it is up to a retail florist to pick and choose which wholesaler works for them. Conversely, if there are not many wholesale warehouses in your locale, you will have to work out a deal to make sure the wholesale receives stock you need for your store.

When it comes to wholesale deliveries, these florists need to make sure their refrigeration is in top shape. The delivery truck should be well-prepared, as should the coolers at the warehouse. Keeping your perishable product as fresh as possible is imperative to wholesale florists. This way, if you get a frantic phone call from one of your retailers, you can swoop in and save the day by making a rush delivery to their shop. Regardless of what type of wholesale warehouse you run, remind yourself that your retailers make your world go round if you are a wholesale florist.

Some floral industry wholesalers do not ever deal directly with flowers, but with flower supplies like vases and pots. If you are a wholesale supplier, make sure your warehouse can accommodate delivery trucks and also florists picking up supplies. Keep your stock nice and neat and make sure you have a good variety of trendy and classic materials to encompass a wider customer base.

Retail Flower Deliveries

Nearly all retail florists get their flowers from a wholesaler. Unless you find a local grower who hand picks them from the field and delivers them to your door step without any problems, using a wholesale florist is the best way to go.

Why? For starters, most wholesalers will stand 100 percent behind their product and have great replacement and refund policies. They also offer flexibility in terms of quantity, bulk pricing, and credit. Wholesalers often offer seminars which allow face-to-face contact with each of their florists. This allows florists to see the product firsthand, ask questions, and gain knowledge on the product they are interested in buying. These are just several of a long list of reasons that most florists use a wholesaler for their flower buying needs. In addition, wholesale florists often deliver fresh flowers right to your door and will also be accommodating for rush orders if you have developed a good relationship.

When you are first choosing your wholesale supplier, be picky. After all, these flowers will be the foundation of your business and the product that your customers see. Look at several different supply warehouses, talk to the staff and management, get a tour of the facilities, and scope out the product. Below is a quick guide on what to look for when you are looking for a wholesale supplier.

For Plants

Check the buds. The buds on their outgoing product should still be closed in a particular manner. They should not be so tight that they are all green, but they should not be fully open. Just a little color peeking out is perfect for a wholesaler's outgoing deliveries. This will ensure that by the time you get the product, it will have plenty of life left for your customers.

Check the leaves. Make sure all leaves are healthy.

Check the water in the transportation vehicles. All the water should appear fresh and have no foul scent or discoloration.

Check the plants' appearance. Look at some of the plants close up. They should be strong with no discoloration. There should also not be evidence that an insect has gotten to them or they have been injured in another manner.

For Supplies

Check out the overall stock. Most supply warehouses should have a good mix of classic and trendy materials and also materials that you will need for arrangements such as wires and foam.

Check for cleanliness. Look around and see if the warehouse appears to be cleaned in a timely manner. If you spot too many vases that have accumulated a layer of dust an inch thick, you might want to move on to the next supply house.

When you have finally chosen your wholesaler and are picking out your own stock, whether it is the plant or supply variety, here are some more tips to follow:

For plants: Concentrate on adding one type of flower or plant at a time and add on from there. Always try to pick the healthiest, most flawless flowers that have the largest number of buds.

For supplies: Make sure that the stock is not damaged and if it does get delivered damaged, make sure you have a return policy in place. Choose a few trendy pieces but do not go overboard. The last thing you want to do is waste money on items that will sit on your shelf for a decade until a trend comes around again. Always make sure you have enough seasonal pieces to keep up with the influx of customers that a holiday will bring.

When you are looking over inventory to see what you need for your next delivery, keep a running list to make picking and choosing easy. That way, you can simply run down the list rather than frantically searching and then having to call back and place a second order because you missed a few items the first time around. When you are ordering hard goods, try to limit your orders to once or twice a month because shipping is regularly costly on these items.

Closing up Shop

After a long day full of customers, deliveries, and flowers, you will almost certainly be exhausted and more than ready to close up shop for the day. No matter how long of a day you have, there are several things you should do before you shutdown so that you can save yourself time for other tasks in the morning.

First, be sure all of your orders are completed and that all the important tasks on your "to do" list have been done. Clean up your workspace and your storefront. The last thing you will feel like doing in the morning is sweeping flower heads off of your counter space and cleaning up that spilled soda from yesterday's last customer. You will also want to take a peek at your schedule for the next day: see what employees are on, what type of orders you have thus far, and incoming deliveries you expect. It might be helpful to have a checklist that is full of general day-to-day operations that you can simply print off and check off as you go. Try to include:

- Opening Tasks

    - Customer Ready Store Front

    - Messages

    - Organizing for the Day

- Cleaning Tasks

    - Bathrooms

- ❀ Coolers

- ❀ Store Front

- ❀ Sweeping the Floors

- ❀ Cleaning Store Front Windows

❀ Errands

- ❀ Delivery Times

- ❀ Pickups (if you go to the market yourself)

- ❀ Supplies

- ❀ Seminars or Classes

❀ Schedule

- ❀ Customer Appointments

- ❀ Which Employees Are Working

- ❀ Prescheduled Arrangements

❀ Sample Deliverable Schedule ❀			
Deliverable	Target Time	Address	Done
Gerber Daisy Displays	7:30 a.m.	Flowertown Hotel	Y
Huebert Wedding Arrangements	8:30 a.m.	University Botanical Garden	
1 Dozen Rose Bouquet	10:00 a.m.	The Breener Residence 14 Flower Lane, Flowertown	
3 Sunflower Arrangements	10:15	100 Flower Lane, Flowertown	
10 Potted Ferns	10:30 a.m.	67 Rose Road, Flowertown	

❧ Sample Customer Appointment Calendar ❧

APRIL 2008

7 MONDAY

10 a.m.   The Huebert's post wedding appointment 1pm

1 p.m.   Rose Breslin and Jamie Boyd

3 p.m.   Eileen picking up arrangements

8 TUESDAY

None

9 WEDNESDAY

10 a.m.   Rose Breslin's confirmation appointment

2 p.m.   Juliette from the Flowertown Hotel on Conferences next week

NOTES:

Ask Huebert's what could have been better and what was better than expected.

The first example above is a simple list form schedule while the second is in calendar format. However you make your schedules, get a standard format for the entire company and stick with it. Each evening, along with your schedules, get a fresh checklist ready for the following day so that you can simply glance at it to know exactly what tomorrow brings.

Lastly, make sure you lock up before you leave. Evenings and wee morning hours are when invasion usually strike so guard your store as best you can.

Employees

Employees are a touchy "should I" or "should I not" type of subject for many florists. On one hand, you could truly use the extra help, not to mention a day off now and then. Conversely, insurance and training will certainly eat up a lot of time and money. If you have come to the point where you can spare the time, money, and patience to recruit employees, it can actually boost your company up a notch. When you are ready to grow your business, hiring a new employee is a step in the right direction.

Hiring

When hiring employees, some things to consider are:

⚘ How can you go about being an Equal Opportunity Employer?

⚘ What will your hiring process entail?

⚘ What are you willing to pay?

Equal Opportunity Employer

Being an Equal Opportunity Employer is easy and necessary. The U.S. Equal Employment Opportunity Commission (EEOC) enforces discrimination laws. It is not hard to follow these laws just by being a fair boss. Simply put, do not rule anyone out because of their color, race, or religion. Do not harass employees. Do not rule someone out because of an impairment or disability. Practice good humanity and being a fair employer will come naturally.

If you do flub up, the EEOC will allow any employee to file a charge with ease, so beware. It might not hurt to research their Web site so you know what is what in the world of equal employment.

Hiring Process

Before you even begin interviewing, think about what you need in regard to your budget and workload. If you just need someone to help here and there, consider hiring a part-timer or an on-call staffer. If you could use a vacation and regular help, full-time employees are almost certainly a better solution. Once you have your ideal candidate in mind, jot down some characteristics you are looking for along with information about workload, part-time or full-time, and set a budget.

Incorporating a hiring process is an ideal way to accurately determine who fits the bill and who does not. Make the hiring process your own. You can do a questionnaire on personality and have ideal answers written down. You can ask the prospect to do an impromptu arrangement. Also, you can simply conduct business in a traditional interview fashion. Whatever you do, make sure it is an organized process that is used on each interviewee to ensure you are getting full information and are treating them all justly.

Salary Base

The best way to figure out a base salary is to ask your accountant to setup a budget and payroll system for you. You can even ask them to maintain it if your budget allows.

Most employees are paid on the fifteenth and last day of the month or on a weekly, biweekly, or monthly basis. If you plan on having employees, make sure you always have enough money to cover their salaries in your account, no excuses. Not paying staffers will certainly result in a tarnished reputation.

Statistic The floral industry is beneficial by providing many jobs. It also has the unique ability to provide for a high level of consumer demand. In addition, according to the American Floral Endowment, it averages $19 billion annually.

When hiring, you will also want to consider your budget and the type of staffers you can hire. If you are only willing to provide minimum wage and part-time hours, be ready for an influx of college kids or retirees looking for some extra spending money. If you want to pay a full-time salary, you may get some prospects that are inclined to be on the same page as you are as far as running the shop.

During the interview process, make sure you are as concise as possible. Try to ask questions that are in depth and will give you a sense of one's character, yet do not get too personal. Here are some sample interview questions to consider:

❀ Sample Interview Questions ❀
How did you become interested in the floral industry?
What type of training do you have?
How did you come across our floral shop?
What did you or do you do for work currently? Describe.
What do you think the most joyful aspects of working here will be?
What do you think will be the most challenging aspects of working here?
Where do you hope that a position in this industry will take you in the future?
What types of arrangements are you familiar with or have you done in the past?
Can you demonstrate an arrangement right now?

Training

All employees need training. No matter how many years they have worked in a flower shop, they will need to adapt to your way of doing things, as it can differ greatly from their last employer's methods.

Orientation

Before you begin training, setup an orientation with each employee. Introduce them to the store and other employees, if applicable. Fill them with enough knowledge that they are comfortable in understanding their position. You will also want to let them know your policies and procedures right away. Many orientations include a small lecture, an employee roundtable discussion, or videos. Whatever way you choose to introduce your employees to your business, make sure you give them a firm understanding of beginner basics and your own rules.

Ongoing Training

Many employers allow staffers to continue their education, which is a wise move. Whenever a seminar or local flower shop pops up, take the opportunity to close the store if you can or give your employees the day off so they can attend. Ongoing training is always a good idea. The more your employees know, the better they can assist you.

Workshops

Workshops are another great way to let your employees bond and gain more knowledge about flowers. Even if it is a wedding arrangement workshop and you do not do floral arrangements, go anyway. You will usually learn something that is easy to apply elsewhere in your business.

Goal Setting

Nobody that ever achieved anything great did it without a specific goal in mind. Goals are the premise of keeping employees on the move and motivated. There are many different types of goals you can apply to your own flower shop. Pick and choose what works best for you.

Sales

For storefront employees, setting sales goals is ideal. Although you can never tell exactly how many customers will come through the door on any given day, by doing some research and looking at the previous year's numbers, you can certainly give a good guess. Do not make the goal so low that there is no incentive to sell, but on the other hand, do not make it so high that it is impossible to reach. Set it at a height just a little bit lower than you would set for yourself. You cannot expect your employees to do more than you can do yourself.

The easiest way to fill employees in on their expected amount is to have a sign-in sheet they initial when they have read their daily numbers. This way, everyone knows what the projected goals are for the day.

Workmanship and Quality

Setting goals in the areas of workmanship and quality may not be an every day thing, but it should be an all the time thing. You can consider what certain employees have to work on and note it on your daily goal sheet, or you can setup a list that applies to everyone — a standard of what type of workmanship and quality you expect out of every employee that walks through your door.

Customer Service

Customer service goals can certainly align with your workmanship and quality goals. You can set daily ones. For example, if you have an employee that never greets customers when they come in, set a goal for him to greet at least half of the next day's customers, or you can write up another customer service goal sheet that includes, "All employees must greet customers when they walk through the door." You can take off or add on to the sheet as you need or want to.

Commitment

These goals may seem daunting or even irritating to employees, but by enforcing them, your employees will make a commitment to do their job and do it the right way. Have commitment discussions that include goals. Ask employees what they think their own strengths and weaknesses are so they can work on them; this will also help you set goals, too. If all employees are committed to working hard to achieve their goals, your store will also reach higher heights.

Motivation

No matter how committed and ready to go employees are in the beginning, many lose steam over time. Even you probably lost a lot of steam since you opened your business, so you cannot blame them. The best way to maintain a high level of commitment and achievement among the ranks is to instill motivation. There are several different ways to keep employees inspired and to keep them focused on achieving their set goals.

Reward System: Setting up some type of reward system, whether it be a free arrangement, a pair of movie tickets, or a day off, will usually keep employees eager to go. Not only will they want to achieve their goals, but they will also want to get the reward.

Good Benefits: Providing your employees with a good set of benefits is also extremely encouraging. Many people have families they must provide for and will pass on your job for one that gives them what they need. If you do not provide quality care for your employees, you should not expect the cream of the crop to want to work for you.

Time Off: Allotting time off for your employees is also a great motivator. You must certainly know how devastating burnout can be, so make sure you give some time off, whether it is for holidays, a week's vacation, or otherwise, to ensure your employees stay fresh and ready to work.

Discounts: Nothing is better to people than a great discount. Allowing your employees a decent discount or even a free weekly bouquet will prompt them to use your services more often. The last thing you want is an employee to buy from a competitor because they are cheaper. Another benefit of giving employee discounts and free flowers is that guests in their home will see your arrangements in all shapes and forms and may also opt for your services.

Qualities of Good Management

While you may put a lot of pressure on your employees to do well, they are putting equal pressure on you to be a good manager. Although they may differ in method, great management often exudes the same leadership qualities that result in great output and respect by those working under them.

When you think of the term "boss," a gangster looking, hard-edged man or a rude, uncaring woman may come to mind. Although these bosses may get results using scare tactics, they certainly are not employee favorites. To gain respect and for employees to like you, you must be considerate and kind. Your employees are only human. You cannot expect a mother of three, an on-call employee, to drop everything on Christmas Eve to help with a large order, and you cannot hold it against her if she cannot.

On the other side of the coin, you must also be firm and disciplined. If the mother of three is constantly blaming her lack of work on her busy schedule, maybe it is time that you two part ways. Being disciplined and fair in the way you handle all employees is only right. After all, you would not let your full-time staff miss work that much, so neither should your busy on-call mother. Being firm does not mean you have to be harsh and cold. Setting rules and sticking to them no matter what will let employees know you mean business, but if one of them breaks a rule, there is no reason to ream them out in front of everyone or fire them on the spot without hearing them out first.

Another great quality to have is quick decision-making skills. This is something you either have or you do not have. If you are lacking in the quick decision department, do not fret. Work on your skills by reading decision skills handbooks and do exercises to improve upon these skills. You may not always be incredibly quick, but you might find that you do not drag out simple questions like, "Do I get the generic or designer toilet paper this week?" If you do have these skills, you are all set. A quick thought process allows you to do things without much thought, providing an air of confidence that your employees and customers will pick up on and benefit from.

Evaluations

When it comes to employees, continuous evaluation is a great way to show you who is cutting the mustard and who is lacking. There are several areas you should consider regarding evaluations, in order for you to see who an effective employee and who is not. Evaluations should be conducted on a regular basis; most businesses do them on semiannually or annually.

Of course, you will want to consider each employee's individual sales and performance. Setting up the same sales and performance appraisal you will use on every employee will better assist you when comparing and contrasting who does what. This appraisal should include total sales and whether the staffer reaches set goals.

Another big evaluation should be on each employee's customer service performance. You could have the best arranger in the world, but if they are nasty to clients, they will never work out. Keep an eye out during evaluation time to see how each employee greets and interacts with each customer. Do they fulfill the customer's needs? Are your customer's leaving satisfied? Can they handle more than one client at a time? Ask yourself these questions and rank them on an A through F scale to see who stands where when it comes to your number one asset — customers.

You may also want to consider an attitude and commitment evaluation. This can be included in the performance appraisal easily or can be something entirely separate. The last thing your busy store needs is a sourpuss employee bringing everyone down or an overly anxious employee who is so hyper they constantly question, not to mention irritate, other employees.

Even if you do not go into detail with evaluations, you should at least take the time to see what type of overall satisfaction each employee brings you. If you are satisfied with their performance overall, that is great. If you are not pleased, you may want to work with them or consider letting them go.

If employees have a poor evaluation, there are some things you can do before you take the leap and fire them. Try to reset some missed goals and see how they perform. Even lower the goals a little bit until they build up to the point you want them at. If employees continue to fail your evaluations, you can opt to suspend them for a while. Send them off with a list of things to consider so they can come back with a new prospective of what you want in mind. If you have an employee that does not seem bothered by their own lack of effort, poor customer service skills, or unsatisfactory performances, you have no choice but to terminate him or her.

Terminating an employee can be difficult. Make sure you let the person down as gently as possible. The last thing you want to do is burn bridges and have the former employee spread bad words in your name around town. Although one-on-ones in a situation like this can be nerve wracking, you owe the person that much. Sit him down and explain why you are terminating him. You can even go as far as providing an evaluation sheet and a mockup of another employee's evaluation to compare and contrast.

Allow him some time to question you as well. Be prepared for feelings of anger or sadness when you let someone go. Try to comfort him as best you can, but if he is becoming overwhelmed, simply say you are sorry for making him feel that way, politely ask him to leave, and let him know you will be more than happy to talk with him again when he has calmed down.

Having and keeping employees can certainly be tough, but you can see yourself through the difficulty by setting strong goals, keeping your staff motivated, and exuding good management qualities.

Customer Service

It is true that customers are your number one priority if you own a floral business. Without them, you would certainly be out of work. When it comes to customers and your store, you want to be one of those flower shops that attracts and also keeps customers. If you can establish and maintain a loyal customer base, your business will be a success.

Customer Base

As we have learned, after you have made the decision to open up a floral shop and before you do anything else, you must consider your customer base. First, is there one? Many times, if there is another well-established flower shop, you may find that a town is not big enough for the both of you. If you do come to find that there are plenty of customers to go around or better yet, that there is no other flower shop in town, the next thing you need to do is figure out a way to round up all of those customers and rope them into your store.

When you are in the process of figuring out your customer base, know that you cannot be everything to every customer and proceed from there. If you tried to get to every single customer out there, it would become quite expensive, not to mention tiresome.

Although there are advantages to any customer base, in the beginning try to gather information about the type of customers you want. Who are they? What do they do on a day-to-day basis? Where do they like to go? What activities do they participate in? Matching yourself up with the right target market can be a critical factor in your success.

After you have established your target market, you can start marketing to them. Telaflora suggests spending a surprising 10 percent on the general public, a higher 30 percent on your chosen target market, and a whopping 60 percent on your existing customer base. You can almost bet on it that you will get an increase in sales if you can maintain loyalty from your existing customer base, so investing the most time and money in them is an appropriate approach.

Wants and Needs

When you have started to market yourself and rounded up a small but loyal customer base, your next step will be to try to figure out their wants and needs.

First up in the hierarchy is needs. What do customers need to come back to your shop repeatedly? Two main components are quality and reliability. If you can combine these two elements each time for every customer, their loyalty is yours.

How do you create quality? Most people just expect quality and become sorely disappointed when they find that it is lacking, especially if they have spent their hard earned money on something they have purchased. At the base of your quality are the flowers themselves. Make sure you only accept the best flora from the best merchants you can find. The arrangement itself and your friendly smile are obviously important, but not as important as how the flowers look and their lifespans.

How do you create reliability? No matter which way they order, your customers will want their order the way they want, in a timely manner. Try to set yourself up with a 24-hour or less time constraint. If people know they can get quality quickly, they will depend on your services in the future.

When it comes to delivery reliability, set up a policy and stick to it. Try to allow yourself a 48-hour turnaround time. Whatever you do, do not set your customers up for disappointment; it is far too easy for them to find another florist for their next delivery. Make sure if you are over your turnaround period, you give them a heads up and maybe a small discount or coupon for the inconvenience. Fulfill your duties in a reliable manner and customers will know they can count on you no matter what.

Next, you will want to figure out what your customers want. They need quality and reliability or they will go elsewhere; this much is obvious. Although, by thinking about what it is that they truly want, you will take your customer duties just a step further and in turn, every customer will get to know and want the little extra you give.

Having said that, what is it that customers truly want? They want perfection and they want speed.

How do you create perfection? Although there is no such thing as absolutely perfect, it does not hurt to try. That being said, you do not have to tear your hair out trying to thread each flower perfectly or making each color match precisely. In this case, perfection is about trying to create a certain air of superiority about your arrangements. That little extra mile with the additional filler they did not ask for, but sets off the bouquet, or that extra five minutes spent tying the ribbon properly and making sure the bow is centered all counts toward perfection. Furthermore, even if you know that something does not match up exactly, as long as the presentation is the best you can make it, your customer will probably never know.

How do you create speed? Most customers today want something when they want it and how they want it, which is most likely right now. Although you certainly cannot be Speedy Gonzalez, whipping up 50 bouquets a day, you can undoubtedly try your best to get all that you can finished as quickly as you can. Conversely, do not let your quality suffer because you are trying to fill more orders than you can properly handle. Take what you can do today and try to build on it each day until you increase your arrangement numbers. It will take time to build speed because quickness will only come with confidence.

If you can incorporate quality, reliability, perfection, and speed into your work, there is almost a solid guarantee that customers will come to your store and stay there for as long as you keep up with their wants and needs.

Types of Customers

There are all types of customers, and with each of these customers comes a separate set of needs and wants. Being prepared for anything is certainly a key to approaching customer service in the world today, but also getting to know each type of potential client never hurts.

Walk-Ins

When it comes to walk-in customers, the first thing they will notice is your store. Presentation is a key element to these types of customers. The outside should reflect the inside while the inside should reflect your businesses core and its products. Use the outside presentation to draw people in and let them know what they can expect once they step through the door. If you want to create a warm, homey atmosphere, create your storefront around that idea. This will help to attract to the kind of walk-in client you want. Conversely, do not have a new trend in the window like organic products if that is not your focus. The last thing you want to do is give the wrong impression and have someone come in, only to be frustrated that your store is not what he or she is looking for. Having a great display on the outside and also the inside will make a good first impression before you even help.

Most walk-ins are the type that have been window shopping or simply strolling along, only to decide that your shop looks like just the place they wanted to stroll into. They are frequently the type that are not looking for anything in particular but can be open to a purchase. By luring them in with a fantastic display, low-priced merchandise, variety, and a friendly smile, there is no way they could possibly leave without an impulse buy.

Greet a walk-in the second they walk through your door. Ask them an open-ended question like "How can I help you today?" The "how" part of the question makes those with manners forced to speak and let you know what they are doing in your store.

Statistic % A study done by the American Floral Endowment shows that by 2010, there will be nearly 20 million United States citizens between the ages of 45 and 65. Luckily for florists, this age bracket also provides the highest consumers of floral arrangements.

If they do not have anything particular in mind, give them something to think about. Show them a variety of lower priced merchandise that they would not mind throwing a few dollars down for. Introduce a new product to make your store seem exciting. Be knowledgeable about everything on the selling floor so you appear on top of things. Allow them to smell or touch a bouquet of your choice to draw their sense in and make your arrangement more appealing. If they still are in a "thanks but no thanks" sort of a mood, step back, but let them know where you will be if they need your guidance.

Once the customer is ready for checkout, try to ask for their name, address, phone, or e-mail so you can send them information on sales and new products as they come up. By keeping them informed, you are more likely to get a repeat purchase. If they decline, still offer a warm smile along with the receipt and fill them in on any up and coming merchandise or holiday specials or features they may want to come back for.

Online Customers

A Web site has the potential to pull in customers that you would have never dreamed you could get. Since the Internet is international, take note that anyone from anywhere can see it at anytime. Knowing this, you will want yours to stand out from the millions of others. Ask yourself prying questions such as, "What would make me click on my Web site versus this one?" Try to incorporate your findings into the Web site building process.

Building a Web site is simple and can be free. Make sure your Web address matches up with your store name as closely as you can manage. By simply registering your name, it is yours to keep and use for further advertising and marketing to draw in a wider range of customers.

If you are not extremely technologically savvy, Florists' Telegraph Deliver (FTD) has got you covered. By purchasing an FTD membership, you can have a Web site linked to theirs simply by providing photos, descriptions, and prices, or you can opt to have a Web designer create the site of your dreams for a small fee.

As for what to put into your Web site, that is easy — anything you want your customer to know. Ask yourself what you try to sell your customer in the store and incorporate it into your Web site. Include holiday information, order deadlines, seasonal specials, hours, care tips, staff information, your design portfolio, and anything else that may be of interest, such as thank you letters from previous clients. You can also include marketing materials like coupons for those that logon regularly or a newsletter that can vary on topics such as the changing season, gardening tips, or a sale.

Having a Web site also opens you up to gathering more client information. Whenever someone e-mails you, save their address and name and include them in on any newsletters or deals letters you send out; always allow for an "opt out" button though. Oddly enough, many clients feel more comfortable typing information into a computer than they would giving it to you face-to-face. Use this to your advantage and gather as much information as you can. You can use this information in many ways. If you see a good majority of those that are using your Web site live in a similar area, try to get a marketing campaign together for that area as quickly as possible to get the neighborhood buzzing and possibly rope in more clients.

Once you have your Web site, updating is crucial. If a client signs on to your Web site and sees that everything is out-of-date, there is a large chance they will not go back because the "reliability" factor has vanished with one click. This also goes for answering e-mails. Since the Internet is such a speedy way to communicate, people will expect a prompt response, which ties in with your "speed" and "reliability" factors.

In addition, what good is a Web site that is not seen? Try to get yourself on as many search engines as possible. Blogs are also a trendy item so if you can, incorporate a blog into your Web site that can fill clients in on daily details and will also expand your "seen and heard" base.

The Internet can open you up to more clients than you ever dreamed of as long as you do it the right way. On the other hand, if you do not take the time to consider what you are putting out there, a Web site can potentially hurt you. So, do yourself a favor and take the time to do it right the first time around, and you might be surprised at what you find.

Phone

A vast majority of your business will come by way of the telephone. Therefore, it is imperative to hit all angles of this potential business getter.

Start by thinking of where most of your clients will have their first encounter with your business: the Yellow Pages. Thus, a great ad is a worthy investment.

Practical Pointer

When answering the phone, always make sure to include the name of your business first and then a pleasant greeting. Before they let you know what they want, customers want to know that they have the right business and that you genuinely want to help them.

Next is the actual call. Whenever the phone rings, make sure you check the tone of your voice. It is easy to let a frazzled afternoon come through the receiver if you are not careful. Make sure everything you need is right there as well. How many times have you called someone only to hear "let me go grab a pen." Although it is a small thing, it is certainly reflective. On the other side of the coin, never having to leave a customer's "side" by having a pad, pen, and order form tied down by the phone will also reflect on you, but in a more positive manner. Start by asking some simple information. Here is a great phone order form to get you started:

❀ Sample Phone Order Form ❀
Today's date: _____
Customer name, address, and phone: _____   _____
Recipient's name, address, and phone if applicable: _____   _____
Occasion (birthday, graduation, funeral, and so forth): _____
Preferred flowers: _____
Vase included? _____
Delivery time and direction if applicable: _____   _____
Price and payment: $ _____

If you find that you need to add on more later to get more useful information from clients, then do so. This is just a great rough draft order form to get you going.

When speaking with phone customers, know that they are at a great disadvantage because they cannot feel your store's atmosphere or see your product and your welcoming smile. Therefore, you have to relay this information over the phone and having good selling skills will help.

Sit down and write a group of adjectives to describe your store and products. Create a vivid image with descriptive words like: fragrant, intense, bright, brilliant, fresh, long-lasting, cheery, warm, classic, modern, and bold.

Next, amp up your selling skills. Do not let the phone ring more than three times before you answer. By letting the phone ring and ring, you are only creating a bad first impression. Fill the customer in with first meeting information such as your name, your shop name, and a friendly greeting; then, let the customer fill you in on their information. Try to fill out as much of your order form as you can without asking questions that the customer has already answered. To make sure you have it right, read the answers back to them.

Take cues from your customer. If they pause after letting you know what they want, they probably want some reassurance. For example, if a grandmother is calling about a granddaughter's birthday and says, "I want something that will make her birthday beautiful and happy," respond with a positive quip that confirms you understand what they want like, "a bright, beautiful bouquet of sunflowers will certainly make her birthday cheery!"

After letting your customer do the talking, take the lead back. Ask common sense questions like "Is this is a surprise? Would you like us to include a birthday card?" Also ask excess questions like, "How about a birthday balloon with that?"

Before hanging up, explain each fee and confirm the

payment method; repeat it to make sure you have it right. Thank the customer by name to make the transaction more personal and reassure them that it will be handled to their standards. Also, always wait for your customer to hang up the telephone before you do.

Big Name Clients

These clients are just as their name states, big. It can be a large corporation that sends flowers for birthdays or a small church that receives fresh flowers for Sunday masses. Tapping into a few big clients can truly make or break your business. These clients also require a different approach than your regular customers. The way you set up funding, delivery, and meetings can vary significantly between each client as well. If you are willing to take on big name clients, you can reap the benefits if you are willing to hand-tailor each business' accounts to their specific needs.

Hotels and Restaurants

Although you may not have noticed before, many hotels and restaurants use fresh flowers for their displays, and they have many places to use them! From the lobby to eating facilities to VIP places; the only limit to your floral expertise is your imagination.

Conversely, getting into work with these places may not be as easy as it seems. Frequently, they will have a contract set up with one or two florists in particular that they will use for their daily deliveries and any special occasions that come up. When the contract runs out, the hotel or restaurant may allow an influx of outsider bids. This is your time to shine and prove to them that you are the best florist for the job.

It is easy to get in touch with management — all you have to do is call and ask. Once you have them on the phone, provide your name and a brief summary about your services. Ask if they have a contract florist. If they do have a contract florist, find out when the contract is up and if they do not, then ask who you can send your proposal to.

You can contract these any way you see fit, as long as the hotel or restaurant is in agreement. A great way is to set up a weekly payment schedule for your standard deliveries and a separate fee for special events.

Here is a great sample proposal to get you started with a hotel or restaurant:

❀ Sample Proposal ❀

Atlantic Florist
123 High Street
Flowertown, FL 55555
555-123-5555

February 25, 2008

Attn: Sarah Sutter, Purchasing Manager

Flowertown Hotel and Restaurant
789 Main Street
Flowertown, FL 55555

Dear Mrs. Sutter,

Thank you for taking the time from your busy schedule to make an appointment with me in regard to your Flowertown Hotel and Restaurant's floral needs. In addition to our meeting and regular "Greetings" package, I am also sending you a proposal. I guarantee that Atlantic Florist's savvy excellence will meet all of your flower wishes to the fullest.

❀ Sample Proposal ❀

You showed me designated areas in need of flowers that included your front foyer and several of the suites. I have included pricing on these areas as well some pricing on some areas in the restaurant that you may want to consider arrangements for. I am also more than willing to fulfill any other requests that Flowertown Hotel & Restaurant may have in store, including meetings, weddings, and other events. I am offering you our full services at a discount of 15 percent off of our regular retail pricing.

Front Foyer:

Product:	Price:
Large arrangement replaced weekly	$175 / week
Freestanding planter for large arrangement	One time fee of $200
Vase arrangement at concierge	$45 / week
Vase arrangement at reception desk	$45 / week
(2) Vases for vase arrangement, if applicable	One time fee of $50 / vase

Suites

Vase arrangement for suite tables (10 suites total)	$35 / week / arrangement
(10) Vases for suite arrangements, if applicable	One time fee of $30 / vase

Flowertown Restaurant

Small table arrangements (20 tables total)	$15 / week / arrangement
(20) Small table vases for table arrangements	One time fee of $25 / vase
Host stand arrangement	$35 / week

Atlantic Florist will also take responsibility for any delivery arrangements incurred throughout the longevity of our contract and any delivery charges for the first 6 months. Atlantic Florist will also take care of placement for the front foyer and restaurant arrangements and will make certain that suite arrangements are given to the appropriate staff members for placement. If any replacements come up before a delivery, Atlantic Florist will replace flowers up to $150 in value.

I truly believe that these prices fall well within the budget we discussed and that our relationship will only grow and become more "fruitful" over time. If you have any questions or concerns, please do not hesitate to contact me at 555-123-5555.

❀ Sample Proposal ❀

Otherwise, I look forward to meeting with you again on March 15, 2008. I look forward to speaking with you soon.

Sincerely,

Christian Boyd

Owner

Atlantic Florists

Once you have gotten an agreement on your proposal you will want the contact person to sign a service agreement to legally bind your contract.

❀ Sample Service Agreement ❀

March 15, 2008

This service agreement is between:

Atlantic Florist
123 High Street
Flowertown, FL 55555
555-123-5555

And:

Flowertown Hotel and Restaurant
789 Main Street
Flowertown, FL 55555

This agreement is understood by both parties to be applicable to all services that are provided to the Flowertown Hotel and Restaurant by Atlantic Florist until March 15, 2009, when the contract will either be A) renewed, or B) terminated upon the agreement of both Flowertown Hotel and Restaurant and Atlantic Florist.

Under this agreement, Atlantic Florist has agreed to:

Provide and place front foyer arrangements weekly for a total of $265.

Provide and place Flowertown Restaurant arrangements biweekly for a total of $600.

Provide and give suite arrangements to the proper employee for placement weekly for a total of $350.

❧ Sample Service Agreement ❧

Provide arrangement on an as-needed basis to events taking place in the Flowertown Hotel and Restaurant. Pricing will be considered in relation to event size.

Will provide replacements if deemed necessary for an upwards of $200 per week.

Will deliver by 11:00 a.m. each Thursday.

Will give a 15 percent discount off our regular retail pricing.

Will deliver free of charge for the first six months of the contract, starting with the first delivery.

Will provide an invoice on the fifteenth of every month to the Purchasing Manager.

Under this agreement, Flowertown Hotel and Restaurant has agreed to:

Provide a 72 hour notice for all event services.

Notify us in a timely manner of any replacements that need to be made and which arrangements they need to be made for.

Agree to use Atlantic Florist for all the hotel and restaurants floral needs.

Agree to recommend Atlantic Florist to customers and event organizers.

Pay its invoices in a timely manner, no later than five days after the receipt date.

Both parties have agreed to give at least three weeks' notice upon termination of this agreement if the termination is for any reason other than reaching the expiration date of the contract.

Signed by:

_____   _____

Sara Sutter, Purchasing Manager   Christian Boyd, Owner/Head Florist

Flowertown Hotel and Restaurant   Atlantic Florists

This agreement can apply to any type of business you may link up with.

Corporations

Large corporations are often willing to dish out the dough to make their building look fresh and clean. They know that a lovely outward appearance will draw people in and often have a florist in place to decorate the lobby and get arrangements together for holiday parties, meetings, and corporate events. Use this knowledge to your advantage and get a list of these types of business in your area.

Once you have a list together, call information and ask who you can speak to about floral arrangements. When you have the right person on the phone, do not just leave it at "we can decorate your reception area." Introduce your product to them in a way they might not have thought about it before — a way that can increase their business. Ask questions like: "Do you use flowers to thank customers for their business or employees for a job well done?"

You can also offer a sample. If they are interested, make sure you include a business card, handwritten note, proposal, and an informative package.

If you are lucky enough to get a meeting, try to get the person to come to your store. This way, you can impress them with other arrangements and products \you offer. On the other hand, most corporate managers will not have a lot of time to spare for you, so make sure you are at their office in a timely manner, bring a free bouquet, offer a discount or free delivery services if you can be their sole florist, and keep the meeting under half an hour. How can they not appreciate everything above — the free flowers, discount offer, and timeliness?

Then, if you are even luckier and receive an offer to join their team, ask to come back so you can get a tour of the building and take photos of the designated areas they want you to work with. You will also want to get an idea of what type of business it is so you can arrange your flowers accordingly. For example, if it is a modern setting, a more contemporary arrangement may be in order.

Hospitals

When you are approaching a hospital, you will want to make sure you follow their rules and regulations since most of the people receiving your arrangements will be patients.

To start, call your local hospital and ask if they have any regulations on arrangements; if so, follow them exactly. The last thing you want is someone to have an allergic reaction to your bouquets. It may also be a smart idea to ask what their room sizes are so you can make an arrangement that will fill the space nicely. While on the phone, ask to speak to the gift shop manager, too.

Make it easy on people to purchase your flowers. If you are within walking to distance, post a sign reading "Hospital flowers!" or something that will draw visitors in. Again, just bear in mind that many of these people will be giving your bundles to patients so make them cheery and as fragrance free as possible.

Local Government

Whether you live in a large metropolitan or a small country

township, try to source yourself to the local government. Many times, government officials do not consider hiring a florist, yet, if you put this timesaving idea in their head, they may just go for it.

Use the same type of premise as you would with a large corporation. Ask similar questions to try to get them to see your service as a time and money saving service for their busy schedules. Show them how flowers can improve their business and employee morale.

If you are having a difficult time tapping into this valuable resource, try to get into your local government firsthand by attending council meetings, donating to charity, and holding community wide events.

Churches and Funeral Homes

These two types of businesses use flowers on a regular basis, even if they are not ordering the arrangements themselves. Although you may not want to directly ask customers, meet the funeral directors and ask if you can provide a sample at the next few funerals or leave a stack of business cards.

 Helpful Hint Many florists chip in a percentage of earnings if a funeral director earns them some business. By giving the director this commission, he will be willing to hand your business cards out to families looking for arrangements.

You can approach local churches in the same manner. Get in touch with the local members of the clergy and ask who does their holiday arrangements. This may lead to wedding ceremony business, and, if the parish has a school, some special events, too.

When it comes to big name clients, know that many more people are going to see your arrangements in these situations than they would at someone's personal home. You will want to provide an air of confidence when trying to fulfill these niches so people can see your service is of value to them.

If you are having difficulty getting business, drive around town to see what you can find. These suggestions certainly are not limited to the mentioned businesses. If you have a town hall, country club, or popular wedding reception site, try to get into these places as well.

When it comes to your proposal, use the most professional business manners you can and always follow up with a call or visit. The best follow-ups will involve a fresh arrangement, another copy of the proposal, and your business card with a personal note. Above all, be kind, courteous, timely, and completely professional; everything you would want from their business in return.

Deliveries

It is a smart idea to offer a delivery service. After all, you almost certainly know the feeling of getting a surprise delivery of flowers to your doorstep. It is most likely one of the reasons you fell head over heels for flowers in the first place. Who would not want their customers to feel the same way?

Types of Delivery

When you think of delivery, you are perhaps imagining you and a loaded truck of flowers going door-to-door throughout the neighborhood. That is most likely not the smartest way to run your business. After all, who will be at the store to answer the phones and make arrangements? Do not fret. There are many options for the florist on the go and the florist who will hand deliver her product.

Carpool

You can opt to get together with other local businesses, preferably florists, and run a delivery pool. You can go at it by either scheduling select times when each business delivers or by asking all the businesses to split the deliveries and go from there. Frequently, they work by having a pool coordinator who keeps track of tags. Tags are given to each item and whoever delivers the item rips off one part and gives the other to the coordinator, who will give them a part of the delivery earnings.

Contracts

For the most part, there are independent contractors who operate their own delivery business. They are regularly paid per delivery and are a great way to outsource your business, especially if you frequently deliver on your own, but are having a particularly busy moment.

Courier

Most courier services will have some basic knowledge on delivering flowers and other types of fragile packages. They will know the delivery area like the back of their hand, but this approach can get costly. Courier services are best used on a small delivery basis.

In-House

The old saying goes, "If you want something done right, you have got to do it yourself." If you are someone who wants things done just so or wants a more personal touch, having an in-house delivery service is most likely your best bet. Furthermore, you can save some money if you can do it yourself. Conversely, doing it yourself can get quite tiring, so once business picks up, it may be wise to consider hiring a part-time delivery driver. If you have an in-house service, you may also want to opt for uniforms or at least instill a dress code.

Taxis

Surprisingly, many taxi services in smaller communities that have little else to do will pick up your orders. The best part is they are yours anytime of the day or not. The bad part is they may not know how to properly transport your arrangements and it could get costly if they stick with their "by distance" rates.

Vehicle

The van is the most prominent florist delivery vehicle. If you deliver far or have a large business, you may want to opt for the refrigerated kind. SUVs (sport utility vehicles) are also a great selection, since they are often incredibly durable and easy to maintain and keep clean.

There are some things you will want to consider before purchase to make sure you get a vehicle that fits your business. That includes:

⚘   What is the fuel efficiency? Big vehicles frequently equal even bigger gas bills.

⚘   Is the size adequate for your delivery needs?

⚘   Can you have it tailored to suit your shop's needs?

⚘   Is there heat and air conditioning, especially if it is not refrigerated?

⚘   Do you need a commercial license to drive it?

⚘   What will the insurance fees amount to?

Once you have your vehicle, keeping up on maintenance is crucial. Always keep up with the oil changes and any other problems that may arise. Try to find a good mechanic who will not dupe you in fees for unnecessary work, but will be trustworthy enough to let you know when a problem is on the horizon. A membership to the American Automobile Association (AAA) is also a good idea.

Unless you are in a pinch, you should not use your own personal vehicles. Not only will they get dirty, you can also get into sticky situations if a legal situation were to arise.

Area Range

Set up an area range you will deliver to and try not to go

beyond its borders. Be extremely upfront with customers about this matter, especially if they are calling from a great distance.

Reliability

When it comes to deliveries, you want to be timely, especially if there is a time slip involved in the arrangement. For example, the delivery must be at the bride's home from a grandmother who was unable to attend before she leaves for the ceremony.

Conversely, you do not have to jump up every time a bouquet is ready to go out the door. Delivering one arrangement at a time would eat up your valuable in store moments. Try to set up select periods throughout the day when you will deliver arrangements that do not have a set time stamp on them. Be upfront with customers about this policy so that they do not become upset or angry when their delivery comes at 6 p.m. rather than 6 a.m.

Fees

With deliveries come additional fees. Most business charge anywhere from $5 to $30 on average for a delivery fee. It is your choice whether you want to determine fees by distance or charge a flat rate for all deliveries. If you do decide that you will go out of your target market for a certain price point, make that extra fee clear to customers that you are traveling the distance for. You can also opt for after hours and priority delivery fees. The more varied your services, the more delivery business you will get.

Above and Beyond

There are many ways to go above and beyond the typical flower shop standards to maintain a great relationship with your customers and community.

Appearance

An outward appearance reflects a lot about the inside. Your building's façade and displays will reflect your store inside. The store inside will reflect your outbound arrangements. Your arrangements reflect you as a florist.

Your store's appearance will also project the given image that your business presents. Are you a country arranger, dealing with cheerful sunflowers and poppies? Or are you more of a classic type, using red roses and baby's breath more often than not? The look of your décor should mirror the type of arrangements you specialize in and the way you want your customers to feel about your store and product.

Staff

Your staff is a critical component to your business. Try to make your staff as knowledgeable as possible and press the importance of a welcoming atmosphere. Even if you have a girl hired to solely work the register, she should have basic knowledge about each flower, hard good, and arrangement in the store. Knowing that you can count on your staff to solve problems in a quick and reliable manner will ease your mind and allow you to concentrate on what you do best.

Investigate

Investigate your customers. Try to go that extra mile and add personal touches. Get to know each of your customers on a first name basis and talk to them about their likes and dislikes as much as possible. The more personal you can get with your customers, the more loyal they will become. For example, if you know the elderly woman around the block comes in every Friday morning for a weekend bouquet, take the time when the temperatures drop to hand deliver her arrangement to her door so she does not have to venture out in the frigid temperatures.

Customer Base

Build up a customer base. There are many computer programs that can store helpful information. Just by looking at what your loyal customers buy on a regular basis can give you an idea for incentives and discounts. You can also alter a program that can fill in information such as customer wants, needs, likes, dislikes, and other information like a favorite flower. You can use this to your advantage by sending a small bouquet of favorite flowers for free to your most loyal customers.

Smile!

Simply put, a smile goes a long way and best of all, smiles are free so give them away!

A Little Something Extra

Add a little something extra and interesting to your

customer service. There are many things you can do to make yourself more appealing than the next florist. For instance, try to get to know something about the business that you can share with customers or use to your advantage like flower meanings. When customers come in and you share what their bouquet really means in terms of the flowers they have chosen, they will have a more fulfilling experience and you will connect on a more personal level. Or if a customer calls in clueless about what they want or need, you can use the same flower meaning knowledge and base their bouquet on information they have given you. For example, if a woman wants to buy a bouquet for her daughter's high school graduation, black eyed Susan's are more appropriate than roses because they mean "encouragement." And again, your customer will be amazed and appreciative that you have given a more sentimental value to their flowers.

Here is a small list of flowers from the Society of American Florists and their meanings to get started:

Flower	Meaning
Alstroemeria	Aspiring
Amaryllis	Dramatic
Anemone	Fragile
Apple Blossom	Promise
Aster	Contentment
Azalea	Abundance
Baby's Breath	Festivity
Bachelor Button	Anticipation
Begonia	Deep Thoughts
Black-Eyed Susan	Encouragement
Camellia	Graciousness

Flower	Meaning
Carnation	
Pink	Gratitude
Red	Flashy
Striped	Refusal
White	Remembrance
Yellow	Cheerful
Chrysanthemum	
Bronze	Excitement
White	Truth
Red	Sharing
Yellow	Secret Admirer
Cosmos	Peaceful
Crocus	Foresight
Daffodil	Chivalry
Delphinium	Boldness
Daisy	Innocence
Freesia	Spirited
Forget-Me-Not	Remember Me Forever
Gardenia	Joy
Geranium	Comfort
Ginger	Proud
Gladiolus	Strength of Character
Heather	Solitude
Hibiscus	Delicate Beauty
Holly	Domestic happiness
Hyacinth	Sincerity
Hydrangea	Perseverance
Iris	Inspiration
Ivy	Fidelity
Jasmine	Grace and Elegance
Larkspur	Beautiful Spirit
Lavender	Distrust
Lilac	First Love

Flower	Meaning
Lily	
Calla	Regal
Casablanca	Celebration
Day	Enthusiasm
Stargazer	Ambition
Lisianthus	Calming
Magnolia	Dignity
Marigold	Desire for Riches
Nasturtium	Patriotism
Orange Blossom	Fertility
Orchid	Delicate Beauty
Pansy	Loving Thoughts
Passion Flower	Passion
Peony	Healing
Poppy	Consolation
Queen Anne's Lace	Delicate Femininity
Ranunculus	Radiant
Rose	
Pink	Friendship
Red	Passionate Love
Red & White	Unity
White	Purity
Yellow	Zealous
Snapdragon	Presumptuous
Star of Bethlehem	Hope
Stephanotis	Good Luck
Statice	Success
Sunflower	Adoration
Sweetpea	Shyness
Tuberose	Pleasure
Tulip	
Pink	Caring
Purple	Royalty

Flower	Meaning
Red	Declaration of Love
White	Forgiveness
Yellow	Hopelessly in Love
Violet	Faithfulness
Wisteria	Steadfast
Yarrow	Good Health
Zinnia	Thoughts of Friends

Customer Loyalty

Maintaining a loyal customer base is the foundation of your business. It is often said that the cost of getting one new customer costs as much as keeping five steadfast ones. As previously mentioned, you should spend 60 percent of your marketing dollars on your loyal customers. Why? If you leave them in the dark, they will most likely find someone else who cares about their needs.

There are several ways to keep customers. First, and perhaps the most obvious way, is to offer steady discounts. By offering discounts by means of coupons or markdowns on the oldest bouquets in your shop, you can gather a regular clientele. Keeping these discounts and your prices steady will also ensure loyalty because consumers will know what they will be paying and what they will be getting for their money as soon as they walk through your door.

By using a customer base and learning all you can about them, you can also hand-tailor extra special discounts, supplies, and incentives for already loyal customers. If you know that the man down the street loves sunflowers, mark it in your customer base program so the next time he comes in, you can inform him on your next sunflower shipment and also some new arrangements you have been cooking up with him in mind.

Finally, hold special events at your store. By opening your shop up to the community, people are going to stop in and feel welcome. You can start small by offering coffee every morning or go big by organizing a charity walkathon that kicks off at your store.

Employee Training

When it comes to your employees, you maybe already know that staff that receives continuous education and service training will be the most knowledgeable and customer-oriented staff in town. Having said that, it is your job to stay on top of their training and to be the kick in the pants they need to strive to be the best they can be. Although it may be difficult, you will also have to weed out the bad eggs. Do not take this part personally. Even though you are perhaps friendly with the staff, you may need to let go. You are running a business — a business that pays your bills.

"Earth laughs in flowers."

Ralph Waldo Emerson

Infinity & Beyond

Starting up and gathering a customer base is certainly a good first step to creating a lucrative business. Though, if you want to go above and beyond the basic business, this will only take you so far. To truly increase you revenue, you have to think ahead and expand your services. Even further in the future is the inevitable thought of what will happen to your business when you are ready to retire. Although you may be just starting out and these thoughts are extremely far off, it never hurts to have long-term goals in mind.

Expansion

There are a variety of directions in which you can expand your business. From a simple location change to a new area of business, like a garden center, you can truly let your creativity shine since you are now incredibly familiar with your industry. Your expansion should closely mirror your current business because, at this point, the last thing you want to do is overhaul what you have already established. Make sure your expansion is something your current customers can enjoy but will also allow you to open your doors to a new customer market.

New Building

Whether you plan on building onto your current location or moving to a new setting entirely, it is one of the easiest ways to expand your business.

If you plan on building on, make sure you build enough that you can grow into the space as your business matures, but not so much that half of it sits idle for years. The precision factor here is crucial so that money, time, and space are not wasted.

If you plan on moving or getting into a second location on top of your current one, hire a commercial real estate agent to show you some properties. You do not necessarily have to go to a space that is a whopping amount bigger than your current one if you do not need it. You can simply move to acquire a space with a better flow or one that uses all of its space better than your current location. The same rules can apply here that applied for building on — do not go somewhere that space sits idle and money is wasted.

Before you move, you will also want to consider the value of your current location. You might not want to move off of Main Street just to acquire a bigger lot. Moving from an esteemed location might also allow the opportunity for another florist to come into your prime spot and take away from your business and customer base.

If you do choose to move your business to a new building or upgrade your current location, capitalize on it. Let all of your clients know your plans and market for your "blowout sale" before your move. At your sale, you can spread the word about the new location and time of the "grand opening." Think of your move as an automatic opportunity to grow your customer base.

Delivery Area

Another incredibly easy way to expand is to extend your delivery area. Build a new marketing campaign around the expansion to let the new area know you are willing to take them on and still deliver the best product around. Keep a close eye on how the new area responds because this will be a good indicator if an additional delivery area expansion in another direction will be well-received.

Business

If you think you are ready to tackle another area of business, then certainly, give it a try because it can be an exceptionally profitable move on your part. Before you dive into a new area of the industry, figure out your own strengths and weaknesses so you can narrow down what will work well for you and what you should not even attempt. Of course, you will also want to research each new discipline by going out in the field and learning as much as you can before you make your final decision.

A garden center might be a great idea for a florist who just loves the idea of flowers in broad-spectrum. You can stock tools, flowers, seedlings, and hard goods like pots and plants to start. You can also grow your own plants and use some of your product in your arrangements if your garden center gets big enough. This will truly provide a homegrown product, which is tied in with the trendy "green" phenomenon that is such a positive association with many people today. Garden centers can also be stocked by a supplier if growing is too much for you to take on at first. Either way, a garden center can certainly provide a needed and fruitful expansion to your business.

If you absolutely love arranging and want to do it on a more grandiose, outdoor scale, then heading in the direction of landscape may be your calling. By opening up a landscaping business, even on a smaller scale, you will be able to sidestep the stuffiness of the daily shop life and enjoy nature in its full glory. In addition, you can show your creative side with the large scale aspect of building unique gardens.

Becoming a supplier is another option for any florist looking to expand. You can take this down many roads as well. Developing a wholesale hard goods supply store will allow you to keep up with your regular floral clients while you have your hard goods supply warehouse on the side. You can also stock some of your hard goods in your store to turn current clients on to them as well. You can also go the road of a wholesale flower supplier by putting up some greenhouses and starting to grow your own stock. There are plenty of options in your own locale, like grocery stores and other florists that will be more than happy to buy local, homegrown products like yours.

Products

Enhancing your products is another way to bring your business to new heights. How you do that is up to you.

You can opt to provide a larger variety of flowers in your arrangements. There are many common flowers like roses, dahlias, hydrangeas, delphiniums, astilbes, and cornflowers that are found in almost any flower shop. You can bump your product up by introducing exciting new colors or by introducing new flowers, exotics in particular. Although they are a little bit hard to care for, many people love exotic flowers, so it may be wise to reserve a corner of your store for your new exotic flower collection.

You can also try to offer a unique product that you do not already have in your store. Dried flowers, greeting cards, candles, and homemade soaps are a good start and something that nearly everyone picking up flowers will appreciate. Think outside of the box and start incorporating a larger range of product within your store.

If you like your selections and do not want to get involved with picking and choosing new products, give your current products a boost. Find a better quality supplier who can give you even fresher flower stock or the latest and greatest in hard goods, if yours does not already. The better the quality and more unique the assortment, the more your business will pick up.

Services

Upping the ante on your services is also another great way

to expand your business without having to delve into a new venture or product.

Customer Loyalty

To start, you can merely offer better services and more discounts. How do you go about this? If you can afford it, hire a new employee or two so that customers get instant gratification when they walk through your door by way of immediate help and the friendliest of service. You can also give new life to your current customer loyalty programs by creating a new coupon program, having more frequent sales, and offering better discounts. Bring your services directly to your clients by way of newsletters and e-mail updates so they are always in the know on what exactly your store is promoting and providing that week.

Programs

Another easy and fun way to breathe new life into your business is to offer unique classes and events at your store. If you do not have the space, find a common meeting place that is relatively inexpensive, but provides a friendly atmosphere for your clients. The most obvious workshops can be in flower arranging, but you can also delve into an arts and crafts style class or how to grow and care for plants and flowers lessons. You can also make a child-friendly class to bring youngsters closer to the joys of flowers. Even more out of the box is to offer something completely unrelated, like a weekly yoga class. If you can clear space in your store and get an inexpensive teacher to come in for an hour a week, you can certainly make good use of your space, plus your clients will love seeing your creative side.

New Niches

As a seasoned florist, you can also open yourself up to new niches that you have not explored yet. If you have not ever done a bridal arrangement or a funeral arrangement, give it a whirl. If customers do not pick up and use your new niche, at least you know you tried and you will not have wasted a lot of time and money trying.

Marketing

It is a fact that, with the right marketing tools, you can certainly increase your revenue and customer base. The question is: how do you use marketing to your benefit? It is worth it to develop effective marketing tools and figure out how to use them to your benefit.

Updated Plan

If you have a marketing strategy already in place, build on it or enhance it. Always stick with the policies and plans that allowed your business to grow to where it is today. These initial plans are what worked for you in the first place and are ultimately your business' foundation.

If you are planning an expansion, you probably have some extra funds you were planning on using for this purpose. It would be wise to take your original marketing strategy to a marketing specialist and have them truly boost your campaign to generate some extra revenue. If you cannot afford to go that far, at least get yourself into a marketing class at your local community college and learn all you can so your next marketing campaign is a profitable success.

New Services and Locations

If you are providing a new service, changing locations, or doing both, make sure you put the word out there with a brand new marketing campaign. Be certain that all of your regular clients know and are provided with the proper information that will allow them to keep coming back to you. A new service or location is also a great way to round up some new customers, so get some new marketing materials like flyers, coupons, and advertisements out there for all to see.

Expanding Your Marketing Area

Another way to increase your profit margin is to simply further your marketing campaign area. You do not have to start marketing to the entire town next door if you do not think you can manage; start small. Pick up a handful of new streets close by your current marketing scope and go from there, or try a new town and see how the people respond to your campaign. If you notice an influx of customers from your new town, then your campaign was a success; if not, keep trying. Marketing is in actuality a fairly inexpensive and easy way to increase your sales and customer base.

Expenses

Of course when you are trying to expand your business, especially in a manner that may use up a lot of your time, effort, and funds, you will want to make sure the move is right for you.

Ask yourself some simple questions like:

What will this expansion cost me in terms of money?
This is a big question. You certainly do not want to put up everything you have worked so hard for, especially if business is booming, only to suffer a big blow or let down when the expansion does not work out. Before you do anything, make sure the expansion idea you have in mind fits in with your budget.

How much time will the expansion take? You do not want an expansion to take away from the business you have already acquired. The last thing you need is for customers to leave your store unsatisfied because you do not have the arrangements you used to because you are so busy with the new building or new craft classes. The best thing to do is see what exact periods of time your current business slows down during the year. You can use this downtime to expand your business without risking much loss.

What type of increase in revenue will this expansion bring? Obviously, you will want to project about how much you expect to realistically bring in with your new venture. The costs should be worthwhile, meaning that it should cover the cost of the new business and then some, so you can pay back any start-up costs you incurred or can put some of the extra cash for the extra effort in your bank account. It simply will not be worthwhile to open a new business that does not generate a significant amount of revenue.

What type of increase in market will this expansion bring? This question can go either way. If you know the town over has had an overwhelming response to your product before, you will have to consider taking on so many more customers. On the other side of the coin, if you are unsure if you will even get enough customers to make the venture worth your while, this too could lead to trouble. Before you start to spread your roots, test the waters in the market you are trying to expand into. Do a temporary delivery schedule in a new location or drop coupons of new products you plan on introducing to see if the response is significant enough to move forward with.

Do you really want to commit to this new obligation? There is no doubt that being a florist can be difficult. Sit down and think before you move forward. Make sure you want to enlarge your marketing campaigns, provide more incentives for loyal customers, and possibly take on double what you are currently taking on. Try not to bite off more than you can chew. If you do, not only will your new venture almost certainly fail, your current business will most likely also suffer the consequences of your overexertion.

These questions will help you to decide if any type of expansion is right for you. If you are content where you are at, do not push yourself to the edge. On the other hand, if you truly think an expansion is right for you and your business, then start heading for the horizon.

Learning from the Competition

There is not a better way to learn about the industry than to watch the competition. Although you cannot sabotage them, you can shop their stores, see what their customers are like, see what their product is like, and try to note what works for them and what does not.

In Short: Still looking for ways to expand community knowledge of your business? How about writing a business related article for a local magazine or newspaper? You can also try to make frequent appearances on your local television station with helpful tips and advice, using your own product as your subject or by hosting a talk session on the local radio station. Get yourself out there in as many creative facets as you possibly can.

If a competitor goes under, do all you can to research why so you can avoid making the same costly mistake. Conversely, if you note that a competitor is doing well, try to find out what is working for them. Even though you cannot use their new slogan, you can borrow some ideas and apply them in your own personal way to your store.

Use every resource to your advantage, including the competition.

Selling

According to the SBA, almost 800,000 businesses will change ownership this year alone and the vast majority of them are small business. If you are thinking about selling your business for any given reason, you will have to do a good bit of research and planning to get the best deal.

First, price out your business to see how much you can get. Using a combination of factors will be the winning formula to pricing it correctly. These factors include:

- ✿ **The value of tangible assets:** These are physically available items like coolers and arranging tables.

- ✿ **The value of intangible assets:** These are all the physically unavailable items like your name and customer list.

- ✿ **Comparables:** These are businesses in your area that are in a location similar to your own. You can compare your business to see how much a similar business sold or is listed for.

- ✿ **Demand:** When browsing comparables you will have to determine if your location is in demand or not. If there are dozens of locations like yours available, yours will not be in high demand. Conversely, if you are the only one, you will most likely be in good shape.

- ✿ **Personal Needs:** You will have to consider the reasons why you are selling. Do you need the money right away or can you wait it out for a few months? If you want to sell quickly, your price will probably suffer a bit.

- ✿ **Buyers:** Consider the kind of buyer you want for your property. It does not mean to get picky and personal. It simply means taking into account a buyer that will want you to fix items to their standards or wants a lower price tag for example.

- ✿ **Appraisals:** In nearly every sale an appraiser will come in and do similar assessments based on comparables, land value, buildings, and equipment. They usually go by tangibles only.

❀ **Taxes:** Taxes will probably take a huge chunk of your selling profits. It might be a worthy investment to seek out the advice of a tax expert so you know just how much that chunk will be.

Once you have come to a price point, clean up shop before officially hanging the sale sign. Make sure it is in prime condition. You will also want to prepare answers for any questions such as monthly electric bills, tax figures, or "how are the neighbors?"

Do not be afraid to seek out buyers once you are officially on the market. Word of mouth is some of the best advertising in the business. On the same note, do not rely solely on this plan. Take out ads in local papers and commercial sale Web sites. You can also hire a realtor who will do most of the leg work for you, but will also get a commission.

When you have found your buyer, negotiate your deal. Figure out key terms of sale such as what you will take with you and what you expect as a down payment. Try to stick to your guns as much as possible but do not lose a deal over the small details. Once the cards are on the table, you will need to ink the deal to make it legal. List all aspects of the sale and pay the fee to have a business lawyer check it over carefully.

The next step is sealing the deal at closing. Before closing, prepare a checklist of all the paperwork you need and the buyer needs. Choose a common location, maybe even a business lawyer's office in case a problem occurs. Arm yourself with all documents, money, alarm codes, keys, customer lists, and any other valuable information that should be seen by your eyes and the buyer's only.

Finally, when all is said and done, it is not. You will still need to file the right paperwork with the IRS. Pick up the IRS Form 8594, the Asset Acquisition Statement, and keep it to file with your tax returns the same year.

Retirement

The definitive decision in your floral career is ultimately retirement. Not only do you have to decide when the time is right, you will also have to have a plan about what will happen to your business once you are retired and no longer running it.

In essence, you have a few choices to make concerning retirement. If you want to truly reap all of the benefits, you can sell your business in its entirety to another florist. Selling the business as a whole, especially to another florist, cuts out a lot of the headache of what to do with all of the old goods, the coolers, and other equipment or products. You can simply gift all of it to the other business owner or include it as part of the sale of the business, and make it their decision as to what they want to keep and what they want to discard. You can also opt to have a blowout sale, trying to sell as much as you can and then sell the property as a commercial ready location, if you own it.

Many families also opt to keep up a family business by passing it on to children or other family members. If your business was lucrative and enjoyable for you, why not pass along the tradition to other loved ones? It will give you much content to see all of your hard work, your "mini empire" so to speak, continue on even after you have retired.

"Where
flowers
bloom so
does hope."

Lady Bird
Johnson

Straight from the Source

There is no better way to learn about the floral business than straight from an experienced florist's mouth. Their words can fill us with hope and inspiration in starting our own business, but also bring us back down to earth about the hardships that can occur in the reality of daily life. Here are some words from florists around the United States.

Case Study: Raymond Brunell

Raymond Brunell, Anytime Flowers, Roselle, New Jersey

"When life gives you lemons, make the sweetest lemonade!"

Florists get into their profession for many different reasons and Mr. Brunell is no exception. His start was quite unique as he fell in love with the business at the tender age of five. As a morning kindergartner, Mr. Brunell began rushing home to meet up with the local mail carrier named Russell. Russell kindly allowed young Raymond to "be his assistant" on the rest of his mail route. Luckily for Mr. Brunell's future security, the last stop was a flower shop.

Case Study: Raymond Brunell

During this time era, the working world was dominated by males. This particular flower shop was not any different from any other business. The air was often filled with cigar smoke and insults as the men played cards in the back room and told lewd stories during break time.

Although it was not the best place for a child, these men took Mr. Brunell in and he soon stopped going with Russell on his mail route, instead rushing right to the flower shop after school. They had him run small errands like picking up coffee and sandwiches at the corner store, always buying Mr. Brunell lunch too. Before he knew it, Mr. Brunell could clean flowers and make a corsage like the best of them and he was still in elementary school!

Mr. Brunell has been in the business ever since and boasts a 40 year resume and counting. Ten years ago he decided to strike out on his own, not knowing the real pitfalls of having his own business but still willing to give it a go. He opened his store with a $50,000 loan from the business' seller and an $8,000 credit card advance, not knowing whether he would be a success.

Over the years he has had ups and downs. One of his fondest and funniest memories was at an outdoor wedding. He had only about five hours to setup for this massive Sunday wedding that started promptly at 11:30 a.m. Arriving very early, Mr. Brunell had no sooner unloaded his first load of fresh flowers when the lawn sprinklers kicked on! Instead of ducking for cover, he worked through the rain, so to speak for 30 minutes. Needless to say when the driver for his store returned with more flowers, he was "soaked to the skin."

Although this is a charming story, it also shows just how unexpected the business can be and how florists must be able to see through the difficulty whether it be with a mouthy customer or an unforeseen sprinkle system.

The "always be prepared" angle is Mr. Brunell's big point and he has some great advice for newbies:

When times get rough and sometimes unpredictable, you always have to persevere and remember to smile.

Know the business from the inside out including the design aspect and the business aspect. That way you are better prepared for the little surprises life throws your way.

Difficult customers expect people to be difficult back. Disarm them and do the opposite — agree, apologize, and act.

The best advertisement is word of mouth, although a television commercial could not hurt.

Case Study: Raymond Brunell

Unexpected things are a part of life.

People use a florist because they want quality and craftsmanship.

Mr. Brunell also truly believes that people use florists because they know they can turn to them if they are unsure. His clients are loyal because he makes sure he sticks with his word by offering farm direct flowers and the best smile in town. His flowers are fresh and the quality is always top notch. He also follows the chain of life treatment to make sure that every flower is completely and properly nourished once they arrive in his shop. Having a backup plan never hurts, too, and as Mr. Brunell says, "Being in such a central of activity here in New Jersey leaves many alternate outlets if the need arises, even if it is the very last minute!"

Touché! It always goes right back to the lovely surprises that life can throw your way!

Case Study: Georgianne Vinicombe

Georgianne Vinicombe

President and founder

Monday Morning Flower & Balloon Co.

111 Main Street,

Princeton, NJ 08540 - 609.520.2005

25 South Main Street

Yardley, PA 19067 - 215.493.1400

www.sendingsmiles.com

www.perfectweddingflowers.com

www.sendingsympathy.com

"Great business minds think alike!"

Like Mr. Brunell, Georgianne came into the floral business by accident. Fortunately, it was "in the cards" for Georgianne and her business.

After graduating high school Georgianne went to Brookdale Community College in Lincroft, New Jersey, first studying communications and then switching to secretarial. During her college years, Georgianne worked full time as a secretary for a large bank

Case Study: Georgianne Vinicombe

in Manhattan. That is where she developed both her typing skills and her love of anything business related. It is also where she learned that she did not want to be a secretary and so she changed her major yet again to management. She graduated with her degree in 1985 and in 1986 opened Mrs. V's Cleaning Service, Inc. She continued going to Brookdale, earning a second degree in small business management in 1988. From 1988 to 1990, she ran both the cleaning service and florist and balloon business side by side before finally winding down the cleaning service. Five years ago, Georgianne's husband joined her on the work front.

Although she had no floral experience whatsoever, her love for the art form of flower arrangements took over. Combined with her strong business background, Georgianne ploughed into the future. In true rags to riches form, her business began in her condo, then to a fifth floor office space, then a first floor office space, until she finally made the jump to retail space. Each time she made money, Georgianne poured it back into the business through inventory, equipment, and better real estate location.

Ten years in the making, Georgianne's store had become so successful that she opened a second location. Even with a $50,000 start-up fee, the use of credit cards, and a line of credit secured by her home, it still took nearly three years for her second business to prevail. But Georgianne never flinched and both businesses remain extremely successful today.

Georgianne's unwavering determination and love of the business is what truly keeps her business flourishing. She claims that those who want to get into the business really have to "do some soul searching to determine why they are doing it. If it is to have flexibility in their schedule or for the money, I believe they will be disappointed. I also think they have to have particular skills to succeed. They must be a self-starter, have a high level of stamina, be able to work long hours, have a supportive family, and be what is known as a 'realistic optimist.' There is no room for pansies in the flower business!"

These skills and traits, alongside near perfect customer service skills, are exactly what Georgianne has and claims to be the fruit of her business. Her advice on customer service is a great guideline to follow for anybody looking to own a booming business with loyal customers. She says:

It's all about the service. Where else can you call late in the day and get a quick gift out same day? Not many businesses offer that. Also, flowers are such emotional gifts. I believe that nothing else can express a sentiment like flowers can. They are such an easy thing to order yet make you seem like you went through so much trouble.

Case Study: Georgianne Vinicombe

I believe the customer is right until they are wrong. I believe that almost all of the time it is best to do everything you can to please the customer but I do not tolerate foul language or verbal abuse of me or my staff. I am firm on this.

We replace arrangements without any argument. I have found that it takes money to have this level of customer service but once you can afford to do it, most customers will be yours for life if they know you stand behind your product.

Customers do not have to call far ahead. We take same day deliveries up until 3 p.m. If someone needs something special, to ensure that we have the product, a day or so notice is fine. We get flowers in almost every day from our wholesalers.

We do not offer packages. For example, all our weddings are done custom and that is what our customers have come to expect. I think what we offer that is special is a very fresh product, delivered promptly and at a fair price. We are open and delivering seven days a week, which is unique in our area. I would say that our service tends to set us apart from other shops.

I think you need to have convenient store hours and the shop needs to be as neat and clean as a pin. It is a pet peeve I have that a lot of flower shops you see are not organized or clean. You must sell through your hard goods within months so that your shop is not merchandised with outdated inventory. I believe that flower shops are very easy to open; they are, however, challenging to keep in business.

Georgianne is also a firm believer in building your business into a brand. Here is some of her best advice on the topic:

Right now most of our advertising budget is spent on Internet advertising. Our Web site is a huge thing for us. I am also very much into branding and spend quite a bit on public relations and marketing.

The key is to always be developing. Always be looking for the next great idea and then acting on it as fast as you can, before your competition. We set business goals (keep our cost of goods to this amount, increase our sales this amount) and because I am so goal oriented, I make sure all associates know what our goals are and that we need to work together to accomplish them. I am probably one of the most goal oriented people you will ever meet.

We have a separate office for our business. It is detached from our main store but it is just a quick walk away. We have not always had one but now it is necessary. Our office doubles as a bridal consultation room and storage for some of our wedding props. We have it divided for the different purposes.

Case Study: Georgianne Vinicombe

Branding yourself is key. A memorable logo is a must. I just redesigned mine after 15 years of having the same one. All my associates wear uniforms. Drivers wear coats and caps with our logo. All our vans are nicely decaled. The floral decal on our vans is on our Web site, our business cards, and so forth. We love hearing that people see our trucks, our drivers, our Web site, and others. We do everything we can to be noticed. We advertise online, we network, we do flowers for high end nonprofit organizations, we go out and visit our corporate accounts and leave them with gifts (with our logo on it, of course). We partner with other business, link to other sites, barter with radio stations, become the official florist for our local baseball team. We do direct mail, thank you notes to senders, invitations to recipients. You name it, we have tried it.

You need a great location in a town that does not already have a lot of florists located there. Nice refrigeration (especially the cooler the customer sees), beautiful fixtures, business cards, a Web site, great signage, a dedicated delivery van or car with decals, cell phones for drivers, a phone system with voice mail, 24-hour phone service, POS computer system (helps with tracking customers and assists with marketing efforts), an office computer with accounting software (such as QuickBooks), nice inventory of containers, and fresh product.

Georgianne also claims that having a supportive family can never hurt. Lucky for her, her husband is a prospering accountant that she says she could never afford otherwise. He quit his position five years ago to help the business as the manager and accountant. Even if your husband is not an accountant, covering all of your basis and hiring a payroll company and an accountant to handle your taxes takes a huge burden off of your shoulders so you can focus on the product and furthering your business.

Following Georgianne's example, by continually developing your brand and marketing, making your location to be the best it can be, and providing the utmost in customer service, you cannot go wrong. Her two successful locations are perfect examples that the proof is in the pudding, or flowers in this case!

Monday Morning Flower & Balloon Co. was founded in 1988 in Princeton, New Jersey and then expanded in 1998 with a second location in Yardley, Pennsylvania. They specialize in weddings and event décor using both flowers and balloons and currently have 20 employees.

Georgianne and her husband have been married for over 22 years and enjoy working in their business together. Many years ago a relative who is a very accurate tarot card reader told her that she would someday be successful in a creative business, which she found hard to believe at the time. Her relative made many other

Case Study: Georgianne Vinicombe

predictions that one by one came to pass, including a thriving creative business. What is the only prediction that has not come true? Georgianne was told she was going to write a book but she claims her contribution to this book is as close to true as this prediction is going to come!

Case Study: Jill Lewko

Jill Lewko, Owner,

An Enchanted Florist at Skippack Village

3907 Skippack Pike #34

Skippack, Pa 19474

Phone: 610 584 7280

www.skippackflorist.com

"Support your local community and always follow the golden rule."

As an art major in college, Jill always knew she wanted to do something creative but she just could not put her finger on it. Later, when her children were young, the stay at home mom was drawn to a "Help Wanted Ad." The ad's sense of humor — "must like dogs and birds" — caught her eye. She went to the interview and the florist handed her a basket and asked her to go at it. Needless to say, to the basket was "horrible" according to Jill. Yet somehow the owner saw potential and the rest, as they say, is history. What was the reason behind the eye catching ad? The owner had her dogs and a cage full of birds in the store, all of which chirped and barked their appreciation for Jill further solidifying her new position.

Jill credits this first job as the most helpful part of breaking into the business. She says it helps to "work for someone that is fully willing to show you the ropes both

Case Study: Jill Lewko

design wise as well as behind the scenes of business practices. That way you are fully aware of the amount of work and labor that this job entails. This also helps prepare you for the very small profit margin most florists make."

Once she decided to strike out on her own, Jill started small and grew — a wise decision after she realized just how much money it took! She said that over the course of two years, the total start-up costs, including a delivery van and full stocked shop, was upward of about $50,000. By starting small and growing with her customer base, Jill did not have to front all $50,000 right away.

Jill also owes her success to the fact that she finds pure delight in helping others through her flower arrangements.

"I advertise my shop with every arrangement that leaves our doors. By making them both the freshest they can be and the most beautiful, in two short years our repeat business is through the roof! I also try very hard to honor any requests from local groups for gift certificates for charity auctions. This is a great way to get exposure and have people come into your shop to redeem their gift certificate. I have a Web site and subscribe to several online order gathering services. These big corporate entities have the capital to advertise nationally and therefore the consumer is drawn to the ease and convenience they offer. The down side of these order gatherers is they take a big chunk of the money spent by the consumer but the upside is they help get our arrangements into local homes. Once in the homes, it is up to our flowers and our stellar customer service to make them lifelong customers of our local shop."

When asked about difficult customers Jill exclaims, "What difficult customers? All of our customers are delightful!" This is a perfect example of the breath of fresh air Jill brings to her local community. Her customer service advice is just as cheerful:

Our policy is to replace any arrangements that a recipient is unhappy with. I think of how I would like to be treated as a consumer and extend the same courtesy to my customers.

Luckily, I have an incredible relationship with my fresh flower wholesaler and we buy only top quality flowers so it is very seldom that we have complaints.

We offer fair market value for both product and labor.

Unparalleled customer service coupled with amazing fresh flowers, arranged into beautiful artful displays, timely delivery, and follow through is what our customers can expect from our service.

Jill also relies on her surrounding community to give her a boost and she does the same in return.

Case Study: Jill Lewko

"Remember, we live and work in our local communities and our reputation rides on happy recipients. By shopping locally, our customers are often supporting local charities and schools that local florists like us are often asked to sponsor in charity events. Our customers' patronage allows us to make generous donations that benefit local residents."

She firmly roots herself in her community by living, shopping, and supporting her local economy. She even tries to keep hiring within the area. When she first opened, she introduced herself by sending arrangements to all the local restaurants, post offices, funeral homes, hair salons, and day spas to say, "Hi! I'm new in the neighborhood." Jill's word of mouth approach and love for her community came back to her tenfold and within two years business was booming.

Loving life and helping all the people that are in it is what keeps Jill and her business going. As she says, "It's very easy to be upbeat and positive when you are doing what you love, surrounded by nature's beauty!"

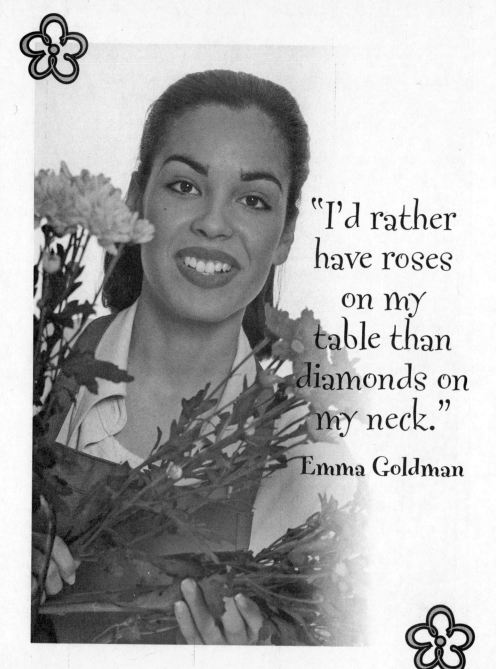

"I'd rather have roses on my table than diamonds on my neck."

Emma Goldman

Conclusion

The floral industry is a fun and fascinating place to be. If you choose a career in the field, you can expect it be exciting and fast paced. Those in the industry must be prepared for the ups and downs that owning a business will undoubtedly bring. Florists must love what they do and have a passion for it, since it takes much time and dedication to run a flourishing business.

It is our sincere hope that this book has taught you something about these things — the preparation, time, dedication, and all the fun and excitement that goes into owning your own floral business. We trust that we have briefed you enough on the ins and outs of flowers as well as the business side of things so you can make the right decisions for you and your business.

From one business to another, best wishes to your new endeavor!

"Can we conceive what humanity would be if it did not know the flowers?"

Maurice Maeterlinck

Appendix of Resources

Here is a collection of some of the best resources out there to get you started. These are not comprehensive; however, they can certainly provide you with the right information to get going. Do your homework and know your stuff and you shall succeed!

National Associations

American Floral Endowment
P.O. Box 945
Edwardsville, IL 62025
(618) 692-0045
www.endowment.org

American Floral Industry Association
P.O. Box 420244
Dallas, TX 75342
(214) 742-2747
www.afia.net

American Institute of Floral Design
721 Light Street
Baltimore, MD 21230
(301) 752-3318
www.aifd.org

American Orchid Society
16700 AOS Lane
Delray Beach, FL 33446
(561) 404-2000
www.orchidweb.org

Association of Floriculture Professionals
2130 Stella Court
Columbus, OH 43215
(614) 487-1117
www.ofa.org

Association of Specialty Cut Flower Growers
MPO Box 268
17 ½ W. College Street
Oberlin, OH 44074
(440) 774-2887
www.ascfg.org

Flower Promotion Organization
(952) 545-7943
www.flowerpossibilities.org

Fresh Produce and Floral Council
16700 Valley View Avenue, Suite 130
La Mirada, CA 90638
(714) 739-0177
www.fpfc.org

Produce Marketing Association
1500 Casho Mill Road
P.O. Box 6036
Newark, DE 19714
(302) 738-7100
www.pma.org

Society of American Florists
1601 Duke Street
Alexandria, VA 22314
(800) 336-4743
www.aboutflowers.com

Wholesale Florist and Florist Supply Association
147 Old Solomons Island Road, Suite 302
Annapolis, MD 21401
(410) 573-0400
www.wffsa.org

State Floral Associations

Alabama State Florists Association
2798 John Hawkins Parkway, Suite 124
Hoover, AL 35244
(205) 989-8001

Alaska State Florists Association
253 Idaho Street
Anchorage, AK 95044
(907) 333-6908

Arizona State Florists Association
850 East Camino Alberca
Tucson, AZ 85718
(520) 742-1409
www.azstateflorists.org

Arkansas State Florists Association
P.O. Box 500
Plumerville, AR 72127
(501) 354-1160

Ozark Florists Association
1111 Garrison Street
Fort Smith, AR 72901
(479) 783-5146

California State Florists Association
1521 I Street
Sacramento, CA 95814
(916) 448-5266

Colorado Greenhouse Growers Association
Wholesale Florists of Colorado
7475 Dakin Street, Suite 540
Denver, CO 80221-6919
(303) 427-8132

Connecticut Florists Association
590 Main Street Bart Center
Monroe, CT 06468
(203) 268-9000

Florida State Florists Association
1612 South Dixie Highway
Lake Worth, FL 33460
(561) 585-9491

Georgia State Florists Association
789 Roswell Street
Marietta, GA 30060
(912) 524-2386

Idaho State Florists Association
715 North Main Street
Pocatello, ID 83204
(208) 232-5476

Illinois State Florists Association
1231 North LaSalle
Ottowa, IL 61350
(800) 416-4732
www.illinoisflorists.org

Indiana State Florists Association
P.O. Box 133
Monrovia, IN 46157
(317) 996-2241

Society of Iowa Florists and Growers
48428 290th Avenue
Rolfe, IA 50581
(712) 848-3251

Kansas State Florists Association
112 South Main Street
Greensburg, KS 67054
(620) 723-2603

Kentucky Florists Association
3954 Cane Run Road
Louisville, KY 40211
(502) 778-1666

Louisiana State Florists Association
224 Hodges Road
Ruston, LA 71270
(318) 255-2671

Maine State Florists Association
216-A Maine Street
Brunswick, ME 04011
(207) 729-8895

Michigan Floral Association
P.O. Box 67
Haslett, MI 48840
(517) 757-0110
www.michiganfloral.org

Minnesota State Florists Association
1536 Woodland Drive
Woodbury, MN 55125
(952) 934-4505

Mississippi State Florists Association
403 Highway 11 North
Ellisville, MS 39437
(601) 477-8381

Montana State Florists Association
P.O. Box 1456
Great Falls, MT 59403
(406) 452-6489

Nebraska Florists Society
1900 SW 22nd Street
Lincoln, NE 68522
(9402) 421-2613

North Nevada Florists Association
519 Ralston Street
Reno, NV 89503
(775) 323-8951

New Hampshire Florists Association
21 Roger Road
Goffstown, NH 03045
(603) 627-8828

New Jersey State Florists Association
88 Fawnridge Drive
Long Valley, NJ 07853
(908) 876-1850

New Mexico State Florists Association
P.O. Box 3342
Roswell, NM 88202
(505) 265-1019

New York Florists Association
249 East 149th Street
Bronx, NY 10451
(718) 585-3060

North Carolina State Florists Association
P.O. Box 41368
Raleigh, NC 27629
(919) 876-0687

Ohio Florists Association
2130 Stella Court #200
Columbus, OH 43215
(614) 487-1117
www.ofa.org

Oklahoma State Florists Association
P.O. Box 614
Drumright, OK 74030
(918) 352-3906

Pennsylvania Floral Industry Association
1924 North Second Street
Harrisburg, PA 17102
(717) 238-0758

Rhode Island Retail Florists Association
820 Boston Neck Road
North Kingstown, RI 02852
(401) 294-9015

South Carolina Florists Association
1663 Russell Street NE
Orangeburg, SC 29115
(803) 534-3780

Tennessee State Florists Association
P.O. Box 240235
Memphis, TN 38124
(901) 323-4521

Texas State Florists Association
P.O. Box 140255
Austin, TX 78714
(512) 834-0361
www.tsfa.org

Central Virginia Florists Association
501 Courthouse Road
Richmond, VA 23236
(804) 378-0700

Washington Florists Association
P.O. Box 1591
Edmond, WA 98020
www.pspf.org

Wisconsin Florists Association
P.O. Box 483
Menomonee Falls, WI 53052
(262) 251-6010

Other Resources

Association of Specialty Cut Flower Growers
MPO Box 268
Oberlin, OH 44074
(444) 774-2435
www.ascfg.org

Extra Touch Florist Association
197 Woodlawn Parkway, 104-280
San Marcos, CA 92069
(888) 419-1515

Flowers Canada
7856 Fifth Line S
Milton, Ontario L9T 2X8
(800) 447-5147
www.flowerscanada.ca

FTD Inc.
3113 Woodcreek Drive
Downers Grove, IL 60515
(800) 767-4000

Teleflora
P.O. Box 30130
Los Angeles, CA 90030
(800) 421-2815
www.myteleflora.com

Flower Shop Network
FG Market
PO Box 786
Paragould, AR 72450
(800) 858-9925
flowershopnetwork.com
fgmarket.com

Trade Magazines

Florist's Review Magazine
Florist's Review Enterprises
P.O. Box 4368
Topeka, KS 66604
(785) 266-0888
A monthly magazine that offers tips to operating a successful business.

Super Floral Retailing
Florist's Review Enterprises
P.O. Box 4368
Topeka, KS 66604
(785) 266-0888
A monthly magazine for supermarket, mass, and high-volume businesses.

Glossary

Accrescent: Enlarging with age.

Achene: A small, dry, one seeded fruit which does not split at maturity.

Acute: Ending in a sharp point.

Adventitious: In an unusual or unexpected place.

Aerial: In the air.

Allelopathic Substances: Chemical compounds produced by plants that affect the interactions between different plants, including microorganisms.

Alternate: Singly along a stem; one leaf or bud at node.

Anthesis: Flowering; when pollination takes place.

Apex: The tip of the flower.

Appressed: Pressed flatly against the surface.

Ascending: Growing upward in an upturned position.

Auricle: Having small ear-shaped lobe or appendage.

Awn: The angle between a leaf and stem.

Axillary: Between the petiole or branch and the stem.

Biedermeier: A tightly arranged nosegay consisting of concentric circles of various differently colored flowers. The blooms are wired into a holder, with one flower variety per ring.

Biennial: A plant which lives two years.

Boutonniere: A single bloom or bud (or several small buds) attached to the left lapel of the jacket. Boutonnieres can be worn by grooms, attendants, ushers, and the bride's and groom's fathers.

Bract: A small leaf-like structure below a flower.

Calyx: The outer parts of a flower composed of usually leaf-like parts called sepals.

Candelabra: A floral centerpiece created at the base, neck, or top of a multi-armed candelabra. Such a centerpiece is usually touched with flowing greens or ribbons, depending on the wedding's style.

Capillary: Hairlike, slender, and thread-like.

Cascade: A waterfall-like spill of blooms, often composed of ivy and long-stemmed flowers, wired to cascade gracefully over the bride's hands.

Caudex: The main stem of a plant at or just below the ground surface.

Chlorophyll: The green coloring matter of plants.

Clasping: Blade of the leaf extending past and surrounding the stem.

Classic Bouquet: A dense bunch of blooms that can be anchored in a bouquet holder, wired, or hand-tied.

Clavate: Club-shaped.

Composite: A handmade creation in which different petals or buds are wired together on a single stem to create the illusion of a giant flower.

Conical: Cone-shaped.

Cordate: Heart-shaped.

Corolla: The petals of a flower surrounding the stamens and pistil.

Corsage: A single bloom (or small cluster of blooms) arranged against a lace or tulle doily and/or accented with ribbon. Corsages come in pin-on, wrist, and hand-held styles, and are typically worn by prom-goers, mothers-of-the-bride/groom, fathers-of-the-bride/groom and the groom.

Crenate: With rounded teeth; scalloped.

Crescent: Composed of one full flower and a flowering stem, often orchids, wired together to form a slender handle that can be held in one hand. Designed as either a full crescent — a half circle with a central flower and blossoms emanating from two sides — or a semi-crescent, which has only one trailing stem.

Cut Flowers: Flowers that are sold by the stem in comparison to live flowers sold as plants.

Cylindrical: Having the form or shape of a cylinder.

Cyme: A short and broad, somewhat flat-topped flower cluster in which the central flower blooms first.

Dais: The centerpiece at the head table (where bride and groom are seated), which drapes to the front of the table for visual effect.

Deciduous: Leaves falling at maturity or the end of a growing season.

Decompound: Divided into compound divisions.

Decumbant: Lying on the ground at the base, but rising at the tip.

Depauperate: Stunted.

Dimorphic: Occurring in two distinct forms.

Disbud: Removal of excess buds to achieve a single, higher quality flower.

Disk Flower: A tubular flower in members of the sunflower family.

Elliptic: Oval or oblong with rounded ends and more than twice as long as broad.

Entire: Leaf margins that are not cut or toothed.

Ethylene Gas: Decomposing leaves and flowers, along with fruits and vegetables can emit ethylene gas. Cut flowers exposed to ethylene gas will have a shortened vase life. Plants such as bromeliads are exposed to ethylene gas to promote flowering.

Filament: Anther-bearing stalk of a stamen; thread.

Floret: One of the closely clustered small flowers that make up the flower head of a composite flower: Grass flower consisting of a lemma, palea, stamens, and/or pistil.

Frond: The leaf of a fern.

Farmer's Market: A market that sells fresh products, like flowers.

Filler Flowers: Filler flowers are used to fill in and soften arrangements. These flowers are generally placed in the lower regions of the arrangement. "Baby's breath" and "statice" are examples of filler flowers.

Fish Bowl: Low centerpiece style that consists of flowers clustered in a glass bowl.

Fixative: Fixatives are fine aerosol sprays used to glue or hold fragile, fine stemmed or delicate dried flowers together. It helps to reduce breakage.

Form Flowers: Form flowers have distinct shapes. They are used as the focal point of an arrangement. Many form flowers can be arranged with other flowers or arranged alone. "Stargazer Lilies" or "Asiatic Lilies" are examples of form flowers.

Florist: A person who sells flowers for a living.

Focus Group: A marketing tool that uses a small assembly of people representative of the customer base that gives feedback on products and services.

Garden: Centerpiece featuring abstract wildflowers. The composition is airy and less full than other designs. Lisianthus, hollyhock, rambling roses, digitalis, and smilax are well suited to this arrangement style.

Garland: Elaborately woven rope or strand arrangement typically used to adorn pews and doorways. A garland can also be paraded down the aisle by two or three children.

Greenhouse: An operation that grows and sells live plants.

Glabrous: Smooth; without hairs.

Glume: Bract at the base of a grass spikelet.

Guard Petals: An outer layer of protective petals found on roses.

Indehiscent: Not opening at maturity.

Inflorescence: The flowering part of the plant.

Involucre: A circle of bracts under a flower cluster.

Huppah: A wedding canopy decorated with flowers that is an integral part of the traditional Jewish ceremony.

Hybrids: Hybrids are plants created by man, by crossing two naturally occurring species to develop a more vigorous plant. This results in a hybrid plant with enhanced leaf or flower shapes, coloration, or growth habits.

Hydration: Getting cut flowers to their proper moisture status to maintain a longer lifespan.

Ikebana: The Japanese art of flower arranging.

Impulse Items: Items in a retail store that are not seemingly a part of a customer's planned purchase. These items are often found near check out and customers often buy them on a whim.

Independent Contractors: Freelancers; people who are self-employed and often work contract to contract.

Keel: A ridge; the two united front petals of a flower.

Lanceolate: Lance-shaped.

Leaflet: One small blade of a compound leaf.

Ligule: A thin, membranous outgrowth or fringe of hairs from the base of the blade of most grasses.

Linear: Long and narrow with parallel sides.

Line Flowers: Line flowers are generally stems that have a tall, narrow columnar spike of flowers. They can be used to give an arrangement a feel of height, or to create a vertical appearance. "Liatris" and "delphiniums" are examples of line flowers.

Lobed: Cut into shallow segments.

Mass Flowers: Mass flowers have a single stem with one flower head. They are used as the focal point of an arrangement. "Roses" or "carnations" are examples of mass flowers.

Membranous: Thin and transparent.

Midrib: Central vein of a leaf.

Multifloreated: Many flowered.

Niche: A specialty or specialty service.

Nosegays: Small, round bouquets, approximately 16 to 18 inches in diameter, composed of densely packed round flowers, greenery, and occasionally herbs. Nosegays are wired or tied together.

Nursery: An operation that grows plants, trees, and flowers from seed and sells them live.

Oasis: Special foam used in flower arrangements. Oasis fits in a bouquet holder and retains water like a sponge, hydrating flowers for extended time periods.

Obicualar: Circular.

Oblanceolate: Lance-shaped, tapering at both ends with the broadest part at tip end.

Obovoid: Egg-shaped with broader part at the top.

Opposite: Arranged on the same node at the opposite side of the stem.

Orbicular: Circular.

Ovary: The seed-bearing part of the pistil.

Ovate: Egg-shaped with broader part at base.

Palmate: Spreading, like the fingers from the palm.

Panicle: Loose, irregularly compound flowering part of plant with flowers borne on individual stalks.

Pappus: Bristles, scales, awns, or short crown at tip of achene in flowers of sunflower family.

Pedicel: Stalk of a single flower.

Peduncle: Stalk of a flower cluster or individual solitary flower.

Perennial: A plant living more that two years.

Perfect Flower: Having both stamens and pistils in the same flower.

Petiole: Stem or stalk of a leaf.

Phloem: Food transporting tissue of a plant.

Pinnate: Arising from several different points along sides of an axis.

Pinnatifid: Pinnately cleft.

Pistillate: Bearing pistils, but no stamen.

Pomander: A bloom-covered ball suspended from a ribbon. Ideal for child attendants.

Posies: Smaller than nosegays but similar in design, posies often include extras like ribbons or silk flowers. Perfect for little hands.

Prostrate: Lying against the ground.

Pubescent: Covered with hairs.

Presentation: Also known as the pageant bouquet, this is a bunch of long-stemmed flowers cradled in the bride's arms.

Raceme: Arrangement of flowers along a stem on individual stalks about equal in length.

Rachis: The main stem bearing flowers or leaves.

Ray Flower: Marginal petal-like flowers of some composites.

Receptacle: The part of the stem to which the flower is attached.

Reach-in: A type of cooler on the sales floor that a florist or customer can simply open and grab the arrangement or flowers of their choice; these coolers are also used to store cut flowers.

Reflexed: Turned abruptly downward or backward.

Reticulate: Net-like.

Rhizomatous: Having rhizomes.

Rhyzome: Underground stem, usually lateral, sending out shoots above ground and roots below.

Rossete: Compact cluster of leaves arranged in an often basal circle.

Rugose: Wrinkled.

Scale: Thin, dry membrane, usually foliar.

Sepal: One division of the calyx.

Serrate: Saw-toothed, with sharp, forward-pointing teeth.

Service Contract: A legal agreement between two parties; one provides services, like landscaping, and one provides a form of payment.

Sessile: Without stalk.

Sheath: Lower part of the leaf which surrounds the stem.

Sidelines: Extras in a flower shop that are not directly related to flowers, like greeting cards or pens.

Silicle: A short silique, almost equally as long as wide.

Silique: Elongated capsule with a septum separating two halves.

Simple Leaves: Unbranched, not compound.

Spadix: A fleshy growth that extends from flowers, resembling a tail.

Spatulate: Spoon-shaped, narrow at base, and wide at apex.

Spike: A usually long inflorescence with sessile flowers.

Spikelet: Small or secondary spike; flower cluster in grasses consisting of usually two glumes and one or more florets.

Spinose: Full of spines.

Spoilage: The terminology used for inventory that perishes before it is used.

Stamen: The pollen-bearing organ of a flowering plant.

Staminate: Having stamens, but no pistil.

Stellate: Star-shaped.

Stigma: Part of the pistil that receives the pollen.

Stock Rotation: Using oldest inventory first; in terms of a florist, you would rotate your oldest flowers to the front of the reach-in, for example, so that they sell first.

Stolon: A horizontal stem which roots at the nodes.

Storefront: The area of your store that is visible from the street; the façade.

Striate: Marked with parallel lines or ridges.

Subtended: Underneath, directly below, and close to.

Succulent: Fleshy.

Taped and Wired: Arranging technique for bouquets, boutonnieres, headpieces, and wreaths. The head of a flower is cut from the stem and attached to a wire, which is then wrapped with floral tape. Taped and wired flowers are more easily maneuvered into shapes and styles.

Terete: Circular in cross-section.

Toothed: Sawteeth-like projections on the margins of the blade.

Topiary: Flowers or foliage trimmed into geometric shapes, often resembling miniature trees or animals.

Tossing: This copy of the bridal bouquet is used solely for the bouquet toss ritual.

Trellis: A woven wooden frame used as a screen or support for climbing plants and flowers.

Tuberous: Like a tuber or producing tubers.

Tufted: In compact clusters.

Tussy Mussy: From the Victorian era, a tussy mussy is a posy carried in a small, metallic, hand-held vase. Today, the term is often used in reference to the holder itself.

Umbel: A flat or rounded flower cluster in which the stalks radiate from the same point, like the ribs of an umbrella.

Undercapitalization: Not starting a business with the correct amount of capital to keep momentum until it generates its own revenue and profit.

Utricle: Small, inflated, one-seeded, usually indehiscent fruit.

Veins: Ribs of a leaf; vascular bundles on a leaf.

Walk-in: A large refrigeration unit that is big enough to walk in and is usually situated in the back of the store; and/or business from customers who walk in the door unexpectedly as opposed to calling ahead or ordering ahead.

Wing: A thin, membranous extension of a leaf blade.

Wreath: A ring of flowers or other decorative materials that can function as a centerpiece, headpiece, or door hanger.

Glossary of Flowers

Every florist must know at least the basic flowers to start but to succeed, knowing everything there is to know about your product is a key element to being victorious. Here is a comprehensive guide of flowers and plants that every florist should know:

Agapanthus: Though available in white, this flower is most often seen in a pale purple-blue shade. Dozens of star-shaped blossoms collect in the appearance of one round flower on a bright green, leafless stem. It is a hearty flower that can be used in centerpieces and blooms in the summer.

Alstroemeria: Also called Peruvian or Inca lily. These small, bright, freckled lilies bloom in clusters, and are available in yellow, orange, pink, red, purple, and white. Blossoms often contain several colors. Naturally blooming in spring and summer, these flowers are now available all year.

Amaryllis: Very large blooms. With two flowers per succulent thick stem, Amaryllis is a dramatic addition to any table. They can be featured in bouquets, though their size limits the number that can be used. Colors include white, red, pink, orange, and salmon. Also available in striped varieties. Year-round availability.

Anemone: Available in white and vibrant shades of blue, red, violet, and yellow, these flowers resemble thick-stemmed poppies. They are widely available from spring through fall.

Anthurium: Also called tailflower. This dramatic, tropical flower consists of a single, glossy petal in the shape of an artist's palette with a bright yellow stamen rising from the middle. Most commonly seen in bright, fire engine red, they are also available in pink and white.

Apple blossom: The white blossoms of the apple tree are available for a short time in early spring. These delicate flowers are usually presented on a branch and are prone to drop easily. The lovely branches are best used as room decorations in places where they cannot be moved or knocked over.

Artemesia: This green foliage with a strong fragrance is generally used as filler in table arrangements. The green is usually available year-round for a nominal charge, though florists often include it gratis in their arrangements.

Aster: A small-bloomed flower, similar in look to a daisy, asters are usually available in white, pink, rose, and purple. This is a well-priced, hearty summer flower.

Astilbe: This flower is generally used as a filler, and can last up to 10 days. Its color ranges from a creamy white to a variety of pinks. Available year-round.

Azalea: Small bush producing vibrantly colored profuse blossoms. It is usually seen as a garden border plant but can also be presented in pots as location decoration. Bloom in late spring and early summer. The most common colors are fuchsia, a range of pinks, red, and white.

Baby's Breath: Fine, delicate, white flowers usually used as filler. The flowers bloom from a profusion of tiny branches growing off a central stem. An inexpensive flower, baby's breath is available year-round at any florist.

Bachelor Button: Available in white, pink, red, and blue. They resemble tiny bright carnations and are used to punctuate larger arrangements. Available in summer.

Begonia: Usually seen as a garden border plant, begonias are available in a wide range of colors. The thick waxy leaves and stems are usually a purplish-red and the blooms are commonly pink, though they are available in red, orange, and white. They are best for decoration and can also be used in centerpieces. Available spring through fall.

Bells-of-Ireland: These flowers grow in evenly-spaced clusters along a single, tapering stem. The flowers are the color of a granny smith apple and are shaped like bells. They are very sturdy and long-lasting. Watch out for the occasional thorn.

Birch: A tree whose branches and logs usually feature a beautiful white bark. Young switches of birch can be a deep purple and serve as lovely location decorations alone or as part of large flower arrangements.

Bird of Paradise: Each of these large, bright-orange tropical flowers is reminiscent of a bird's wing. The orange blooms are streaked with purple and white and sit atop thick, sturdy stalks. Because of their size and weight, these flowers are far better suited for table arrangements than bridal bouquets.

Bleeding Heart: A flowering plant usually seen in border gardens but also used in potted arrangements. The plants feature deep-pink, drooping, heart-shaped flowers. These would be lovely as location decorations particularly for a wedding set in a garden.

Bluebell: These bell-shaped flowers grow 12 to 24 inches high, with the blooms clustered closely together. The flowers bloom in spring and usually die off by mid-to-late summer. Due to the fleeting nature of the blooming time, these flowers are not easily found nationwide.

Bouvardia: A small tubular flower with a starburst of petals. Usually found in brilliant snow white, bouvardia also comes in pink and red varieties. This flower is most often used as an accent or background flower in bridal bouquets. Available in spring and summer.

Boxwood: Often referred to simply as "box," this greenery is used as filler for table arrangements and bouquets. Branches of sturdy box bear small, dark-green leaves and can work well to support heavier arrangements.

Calla Lily: These flowers have a thick, white, cone-shaped petal with a yellow stamen. They occur one bloom to a stem and may last for several weeks with a change of water. The stems are thick and bright green. A smaller variety is also available, occurring in hues from pink to cranberry and yellow. Available from spring through fall.

Calcynia: Tiny, white, star-shaped flowers occurring among dark-green leaves, these delicate flowers add a light touch to a bridal bouquet. Available year-round.

Camellia: With beautiful dark-green, waxy leaves and rose-size blooms, the camellia is a stunning flower. Available in a wide variety of colors, the white and pinks are most common. Use the blooming flower and the bud in your bouquet for a different texture. These hearty flowers grow well in pots and can be used on tables or to create colorful borders around the event location. Available from spring through fall.

Camellia Leaf: These beautiful, deep-green leaves accent any arrangement beautifully. They are shiny, waxy, sturdy, and last a long time. They are useful as a support green in any bouquet. Available from spring through fall.

Campanula: The bell-shaped flowers of the campanula give it its common names of bellflower and Canterbury bells. The flowers bloom from a long stem with colors including blue-purple, pink, and white. They bloom in summer and are best used in table arrangements.

Carnation: Also known as dianthus, carnations are available in almost any color and in several sizes. These are hearty, long-lasting flowers, and can be dyed to match your color scheme. Purple carnations are particularly fragrant. They are available year-round and are usually inexpensive.

Cattleya Orchid: These orchids are usually found in shades of white, with pink or lavender in the center of each petal. They are larger than more common orchid varieties. Available through florists year-round. Very expensive.

Cherry Blossom: The blossoms of a cherry tree are usually presented as full branches. The small pinkish-white flowers fall very easily and are available only briefly in the spring.

China-berry: Small yellowish-red, hard berries found on branches of the China-berry tree. Thin branches of these brightly colored berries are often included in bouquets to add an accent of color and a distinct texture to the arrangement.

Chrysanthemum: With multiple blooms on each stem, this flower is available in almost every color including white, yellow, red, orange, and purple. The versatile chrysanthemum comes in many shapes and sizes and lasts up to two weeks. Available any time of year.

Clematis: Ranging in color from pink and white to deep purple, this flower of a climbing vine makes a dramatic addition to any bouquet or arrangement. The larger blooms make interesting boutonnieres. Available in summer.

Columbine: With dark-green or gray-green leaves and petals ranging in color from red-pink with soft green tips to yellow, blue, and white, the columbine is a sturdy perennial that grows 24 to 30 inches high and blooms in summer. Its flowers feature spurs of various lengths depending on the variety.

Cosmos: Most commonly available in pink, this flower is reminiscent of a delicate daisy. Its thin stem allows many flowers to be gathered into a single bouquet. The colors available include white and the full range of pinks and purples. The chocolate cosmos, available in a deep reddish-purple hue, is particularly attractive, appearing to be almost the color of chocolate.

Crab Apple Blossom: The white blossoms of the crab apple tree are available for a short time in early spring. These delicate flowers are usually presented on a branch and are prone to drop easily. The lovely branches are best used as room decorations in places where they cannot be moved or knocked.

Cymbidium Orchid: Breathtaking, but very pricey, cymbidium orchids are often used to accent a bouquet. The colors range from chartreuse (a vibrant green) to white to hot pink. The centers of the flower also vary in color. Due to their price and fragility, these flowers are more suitable for bouquets, boutonnieres, and corsages than for table arrangements.

Daffodil: This widely-available yellow flower can add a cheery feel to any event. If you are a daffodil fan, you should note that they are generally not available after the first few months of spring.

Dahlia: These affordable, full-blossomed flowers are available in a wide range of colors from pale pinks to dramatic, dark reds. They are inexpensive and are perfect for small bouquets and bright centerpieces. Available summer through fall.

Daisy: Usually white or yellow with yellow centers. These popular flowers with little scent are inexpensive, any time. Daisies are hearty and can last more than a week. Available summer through fall.

Day Lily: Usually available in shades of cream, orange, red, and yellow with a variety of stem lengths. This flower is not ideal for bouquets but is perfect for use in centerpieces and other decorative arrangements. Available spring through fall.

Delphinium: Usually found in blue, white, rose, or lavender. Long stocks covered with delicate blossoms and lacy foliage. Delphinium requires a lot of water and is particularly lovely in vase arrangements. Many brides include some delphinium in their bouquets as part of the "something blue" tradition. Available spring through fall.

Dendrobium Orchid: Available in colors ranging from pinks to purples, this orchid grows in long branches featuring dozens of perfect blooms. It is the least pricey and heartiest member of the orchid group.

Dogwood: Like apple and cherry blossoms, dogwood flowers are available only for a short time in early spring and are delicate. Ranging from light pink to white, they are usually presented on a branch and would serve best as room decorations rather than as centerpieces because of their delicate nature.

Eucalyptus: The leaves and small branches of any of the eucalyptus varieties make excellent greenery for arrangements. Certain varieties such as baby blue are extremely fragrant. Seeded eucalyptus, which resembles non-blooming lilac, makes an excellent filler addition.

Euphorbia: Small white flowers with open, white blossoms. They gather in a round grouping and are usually used as an accent in bouquets. Be careful, the sap of this plant can irritate your skin. Available year-round in warmer climates.

Fern: A versatile, green, non-flowering plant with long leafy fronds. Add greenery to any location or bouquet with this plant. They are hearty and will last for months if properly watered.

Forget-me-not: A dainty blue flower with yellow or white centers. Perfect for small posies and delicate table arrangements. This flower is available in the spring and is often difficult to find.

Forsythia: A woody green bush often trained into hedges. Blooms in early spring with vibrant yellow blossoms. When blooming, these tall branches can be cut and used for location decoration. Unlike the blossoms of fruit trees, these branches are hearty and long-lasting when cut.

Foxglove: A funnel-shaped summer blossom of soft golden-brown and white, with certain varieties featuring pink highlights. The leaves are olive-green to medium-green, and the plant grows from 30 inches to four feet high, with a one-foot spread. An unusual addition to any arrangement.

Freesia: These fragrant small flowers are often used in wedding bouquets and table arrangements. They are usually found with several blooms per stem. Their color range is wide, including purple, yellow, white, and pink, making this a versatile wedding flower. Once cut, freesia can live five to 10 days.

French Tulip: This is the largest of all the tulips, and like its smaller cousins, these flowers are available in almost any color you can imagine, including striped varieties. Though they are quite delicate and sensitive to heat and lack of water, French tulips are used widely in wedding arrangements. They last seven to 10 days.

Galax Leaf: Shiny, waxy, dark-green leaves used as filler in arrangements or as accents in any bouquet. The leaves are sturdy, long-lasting, and always available.

Gardenia: Each gardenia is a single white bloom about three to four inches across and surrounded by dark green leaves. They are extremely fragrant, and the petals bruise easily. Quite expensive. Available in spring and summer.

Geranium: A hearty green plant with vibrantly colored blooms ranging in color from white to pinks and the classic bright red. The blooms occur in round collections at the end of the stems. The broad mid-green leaves are often used as a fresh-smelling base in bouquets.

Gerbera: Also called gerber daisy. This large bloom has single or double ring of thin petals, and a sturdy, bright-green stalk. Available in almost every color imaginable, from the hottest pinks and yellows, to reds and oranges, just to name a few.

Ginger: A dramatic, large, tropical flower occurring in a brush-like fashion at the end of a sturdy, thick green stalk. Best for tall flower arrangements. Ginger is most often red, but also occurs in pink. They may be pricey in colder regions.

Gladiolus: A great flower for cutting, gladiolus is notable for its sword-shaped leaves, which explains its other commonly used names, sword lilies and corn lilies. Gladiolus comes in virtually every color except blue, and can be bi- or tri-colored. The plant can grow from two to six feet in height, while the flowers range from one to eight inches in diameter. The flowers are readily available in summer and generally last seven to 10 days.

Goldenrod: For years this bright gold plant was only seen as a weed to be avoided because many people are allergic to it. If allergies are not a problem, these fluffy flowers make a bright addition to your bouquet.

Grape Leaf: A large triangular green leaf with textured veins and ruffled edges. They are decorative simply placed on tabletops or used in arrangements. And as a bonus, they are edible. Available in summer.

Heather: An evergreen shrub, with certain varieties reaching two feet high, featuring small leaves and spikes and tiny flowers. Heather blooms from summer until late fall. The flowers come in many different shades of pink, from a purple-pink to rose pink to mauve.

Hyacinth: A spring blossom with bright green leaves and a very thick stem, grown from a bulb. The cluster of blossoms begins mid-stalk and tapers toward the top. Extremely fragrant, hyacinth is available in shades of pink, white, blue, yellow, and red.

Hydrangea: A shrub featuring flowers in the form of large globes made up of clusters of small blooms. Most commonly seen in hues of purple and blue, the colors vary to include white and bright red. Some varieties have two-tone petals, some are speckled or striped. Depending on the variety, the flowers bloom from mid-summer through the fall.

Iris: Available in white, blue, violet, yellow, and orange. A single bloom appears at the end of each long stalk and features several large petals. Available in the spring and blooming all summer long.

Ivy: An inexpensive, climbing, trailing plant with shiny leaves available throughout the year. Ivy leaves vary in size. They usually appear in a deep green, but also occur in a variegated variety with a creamy yellow border. Some ivy produces yellow flowers in the fall.

Jasmine: A sometimes-climbing shrub, with tiny yellow, pale pink, or white star-shaped flowers famous for their fragrance. Both the flowers and the trailing leafy vines are often used in bouquets and table arrangements.

Kale: In the same group of plants as mustard, broccoli, and cauliflower, ornamental kale is a flowering plant with blooms of rose, cream, white, or purple. This plant is most useful in table arrangements and is seldom seen in the bridal bouquet.

Larkspur: These vibrantly colored blossoms appear along tall green spikes. They are available in white, pink, and blue, with some varieties having an overlay of a second color, such as yellow. Larkspur blooms in early to mid-summer, and the leaves are soft green to bright green. Some dwarf varieties grow to only 18 inches high, and certain strains reach eight feet in height.

Laurel: Dark green leaves of a shrub used as greenery in bouquets and table arrangements. Available year-round.

Lavender: A fragrant mauve flower with dusty green leaves. Its buds grow in the shape of small cones. Lavender is available in several varieties and is a wonderful fragrant addition to any bouquet. Tiny pots of lavender are sometimes used as guest favors.

Lemon Leaf: Leaves of the lemon tree add a bright green touch to bouquets and arrangements. They are hearty and long-lasting, with the bonus of a wonderful citrus scent.

Lilac: Usually available in white or lavender. Sturdy wooden stalks with many tiny flowers. This wonderfully fragrant flower is only available for a brief period in the spring.

Lily: Usually white or cream with tinges of pink or lavender. There are many varieties of lilies, with stargazers and calla lilies being those most commonly used in wedding arrangements. Available spring through summer.

Lily of the Valley: Tiny, white, delicate, bell-shaped flowers appearing in clusters on the end of bright green stems, amid broad flat leaves. As fragrant as they are expensive. These rare flowers are available only for a short time in the spring.

Lisianthus: With the appearance of delicate, papery tulips, these surprisingly hearty flowers are seen in bouquets of all styles. The blooms are available in white, pink, and a purple-blue. They are available virtually year-round, but peak in the summer time.

Magnolia: Large white or light pink, eight-petal blossoms appearing for a short time in early spring. Magnolias are quite dramatic when used in bouquets and arrangement, but be aware, they are delicate.

Maidenhair Fern: Used in many commercial floral arrangements, this feathery fern is usually used as a base over which the flowers are arranged. Available year-round.

Marigold: This familiar flower features large blossoms in varying shades of yellow and orange, with soft green leaves and short stems. Marigold blooms in summer. They are easy to grow and are a bright addition to any arrangement.

Mint: A fragrant, delicious herb with small ridges along its blue-green leaves. Used to brighten the taste of food and drink or add a wonderful fragrance to the bridal bouquet.

Mint is ready for plucking in the spring and is available through the fall.

Muscari: Also known as grape hyacinth, these delicate succulent stems are often gathered for small hand-carried bouquets. Dozens of small blooms begin mid-stem and taper toward the top. Available in white and deep purple-blue.

Myrtle: A fragrant branch-like herb with small flat leaves and white blooms. Myrtle is often used as a dramatic green filler in both bouquets and table arrangements. Available in spring and summer.

Narcissus: Resembling white daffodils, single narcissus blossoms appear at the end of tall, sturdy stalks. They are fragrant and are readily available in the summer and fall.

Nasturtium: Bright orange or yellow flowers grown on vines. These vibrant, papery flowers on thin stems are edible and have a peppery taste. Perfect for cake decoration. Available summer and fall.

Oasis: A malleable, foam-like sponge that serves as the base for flower arrangements. It is soaked in water, and retains moisture to nourish flowers. Stems are poked in the oasis directly.

Orange Blossom: Small clustered white blossoms from orange tree branches. They are fragrant, though the smell of orange is not pervasive. Orange blossom is a traditional wedding flower. Available in spring and summer.

Orchid: Usually white, or in shades of pink, lavender, or yellow. Expensive, but popular and easy to locate. Available year-round through florists (see also cattleya, dendrobium, and phalaenopsis).

Pansy: Small to medium in size, velvety blooms, often with darker color inside. They are available in mixed colors, though purple and yellow are most common. Pansies can be found year-round, and since they are edible, they are ideal decorations for the wedding cake.

Parrot Tulip: Slightly larger and more costly than conventional tulips, these are distinguished by their ruffled, feather-like petals. Available in an array of solid colors, usually in hues of red, yellow, and orange, as well as two-color varieties. Most are readily available in the spring and early summer.

Peony: Large ruffled, round bloom with soft, feathery petals. The colors range from white to a variety of pinks to deep red. These pricey blooms are available in the spring and summer.

Pepperberry: Available as small branches with yellow-tinged red berries. This plant is often used as a colorful filler for bouquets with a wilderness look. Available year-round, this is a particular favorite at holiday weddings.

Periwinkle: An evergreen shrub with small five-petal blooms. Similar in look to stephanotis without the high price tag. They are available in mixed colors throughout the spring and summer.

Phalaneopsis Orchid: Beautiful, elegant phalaneopsis

plants can be used at the center of any table if the budget allows. The blossoms are available in several hues of pink and yellow, though white is most often seen. The petals are broad and flat, making these ideal for boutonnieres.

Phlox: A small, thin-petaled flower that blooms in large clusters. They are available in mixed colors throughout the spring, summer, and fall.

Pittosporum: A green shrub bearing fragrant tiny white flowers that are often used in bouquets as accent and filler. Available spring through fall.

Poppy: Various sized blooms featuring bright, papery petals. The single or double blooms appear individually upon thin stalks. Poppies are available in mixed colors, but are most commonly found in red. Also available are the orange California poppy and the rare blue Himalayan variety. They first appear in spring and bloom through mid-summer.

Queen Anne's Lace: A white-bloomed filler flower usually seen in large arrangements. Not the best for bouquets, but useful in filling empty spaces when the budget will not allow for higher priced flowers. Available year-round at a low cost.

Ranunculus: Large multi-petal bloom resembling a cabbage rose. Their stalks are thin and not particularly sturdy. The color range is astonishing, making them a versatile flower for bridal bouquets. They bloom from spring through the summer.

Rhamnus: Lovely broad, flat leaves available in a dark green year-round. These evergreen leaves are wonderful for the base of a bouquet or in table arrangements.

Rice Flower: A light pink to white spray of tiny round blossoms actually resembling rice, this flower is an elegant filler for bouquets. It adds a lightly fragrant, elegant look.

Rose: Available in a number of colors, rose buds appear at the end of a long, thorny stems. Roses vary in size from six inches across to the miniature variety whose bud is less than one inch across. Naturally, roses are a popular and fragrant wedding flower. Summer is their season, but they are available year-round through florists.

Rosehips: Small russet-colored berries presented on slender branches, rosehips work particularly well when mixed with yellow, orange, burgundy, or red flowers. Available in fall and winter.

Sage: A fragrant herb with soft green to blue-silver leaves. Some variations yield trumpet-shaped blooms in purple, white, red, and pink. Sage can add its soft fragrance to bouquets and enhance any table arrangement.

Salal: Broad, flat, green leaves used in bouquets and table arrangements. Salal also produces small, bell-shaped flowers and berries that can add texture to a bouquet.

Scabiosa: Also called pincushion, this is a long-stemmed bloom with thin petals. A ring of ray petals surrounds an inner circle of petals and berry-like buds. Available in the deepest purples as well as salmon, pink, and white.

Seeded Eucalyptus: If you have seen lilac before it blooms, you will know the look of seeded eucalyptus. Tiny, smooth, pale-green seed pods align and branch off from a single stem. Available year-round.

Smilax: A delicate vine with tiny, waxy, dark green leaves. Smilax vines are often woven together to make beautiful garlands or used at the base of centerpieces. This is an excellent plant to incorporate into a wedding arch or Chuppah for a relaxed romantic feeling. Available year-round. Smilax is a medium to highly-priced green.

Snapdragon: A beautiful summer flower available in a wide variety of colors. The brightly colored blooms of the snapdragons occur along pale green stems which can grow to three feet in height. The more common size ranges between eight to 18 inches. These flowers begin to bloom in late spring.

Snowberry: Lovely leafy branches featuring small berries. This plant is wonderful for creating texture in bouquets and table arrangements. Available in fall and winter.

Springeraii: This feathery, prickly green is commonly used for garland and to fill large, empty spaces in floral arrangements and bouquets. Its color ranges from light to dark green. It is long lasting, inexpensive, and available year-round.

Stargazer Lily: The most expensive of the lily group, these fragrant flowers grow two or three to a stem. The petals are predominantly pink with white edges. The petals are freckled with darker pink. Their bright orange pollen can stain both skin and clothing.

Statice: Clusters of blooms along tall, sturdy stalks. This affordable flower is commonly available year-round in white, purple, and pink.

Stock: Tall, hearty, and affordable flowers featuring multiple blossoms along long, thick, light green stems. The blooms are available in both single and double varieties. The fragrance of stock is quite strong but not entirely pleasant. Best used in table arrangements though it is quite commonly found in bridal bouquets. Available all year in soft hues of white, cream, yellow, and pink.

Sunflower: Large field flower with a ring of ray petals around a dark center. These flowers can range in size from two to 10 inches across, making them a dramatic choice at any wedding. Available in red and yellow.

Sweet William: This small bloom with velvety petals was a favorite in 16th century England. Available in the spring and summer in mixed colors, most commonly pink and blue.

Spray Orchid: This dramatic plant features tiny orchid blossoms that appear along thin, tendril-like branches. This is a winter orchid and falls in the expensive range.

Stephanotis: These are white trumpet-shaped flowers that grow on vines. They are among the most popular and traditional wedding flowers. The high price of this sweet, fragrant flower reflects the fact that each blossom must be removed from its vine and specially prepared for the bouquet. The base of each delicate flower is attached to a small wire and wrapped with floral tape. Most common in summer, but also available in spring and fall.

Straw Flowers: Available in bright white, yellow, orange, and red, strawflower is featured in many bridal bouquets. With multiple, straw-like petals around a yellow center, strawflower looks like a cousin to the common daisy. Available in the summer.

Sweet Pea: A climbing vine that yields medium sized blooms available in many colors and varieties: rose, red, maroon, pink, white, yellow, blue, purple, or bi-colored. This is a vibrant, fragrant flower with a delicate look. Sweet pea is available in the spring.

Tansy: Small button-like flowers. The yellow variety is most common. Tansy is available in the summer.

Tuberose: Trumpet shaped blossoms in pale pink and white appear in clusters along a sturdy, thick, light green stem. This variety has a sweet pervasive smell that will remind you of the tropics. One stem will perfume an entire room. Tuberose has grown in popularity and is now available year-round.

Tulip: Any of an assortment of bulb varieties available in almost every color. Each tall, succulent stem ends with one blossom made of smooth, flat petals. The blooms vary in size from medium to large and are available from early spring through the summer. Tulip varieties also include the ruffled parrot tulip and the large French tulip.

Veronica: This is a long tapered flower, dense with blooms.

Veronica is available in shades of blue, red, and pink and can be found all summer long.

Viburnum: Similar in shape to hydrangea, viburnum is a light green, pompom shaped flower. Each larger flower is made up of a group of smaller blossoms. They are not the best choice for bouquets since they are quite delicate and wilt easily. They are reasonably priced and available in summer.

Violet: Available in white, blue, and most commonly, purple. These tiny delicate flowers have a sweet, subtle fragrance and are available in the spring. Their dramatic color makes them ideal for decorating the wedding cake.

Wax Flower: Clusters of small, waxy flowers available in reds and purples. These hearty, star-shaped blooms hold up well in bridal bouquets and are available in the spring through the fall.

Zephyr Lily: Available in white, yellow, and shades of pink, the zephyr is smaller than most lilies, making it a quaint addition to any bouquet. Zephyrs bloom from the summer through fall.

Zinnia: Available with both single or double blooms, zinnias, with their pointed ray petals, occur in almost every color imaginable. They are both hearty and affordable, and can be found for most of the year.

Author Biography

Stephanie Beener is a freelance writer who is also currently attending the Art Institute of Pittsburgh Online. She currently has a position at AOL where she is gaining experience in her field. Stephanie hopes to graduate from the Art Institute with a bachelor's degree in hand, ready to take the writing world by storm.

Stephanie was recently wed in 2006 to her loving husband Adam in a romantic sunset ceremony. She is also a proud mother of her two year old daughter, Kaylee, and her rescued American Bulldog/Boxer mix, Rocky.

In her free time, Stephanie enjoys reading, writing, DIY home/garden projects, and fun in the sun with her family.

Index